CREATIVE COPING SKILLS FOR
TEENS AND TWEENS

by the same author

Toxins and Antidotes
A Therapeutic Card Deck for Exploring Life Experiences
Bonnie Thomas
Illustrated by Rosy Salaman
ISBN 978 1 78592 763 8

Creative Expression Activities for Teens
Exploring Identity through Art, Craft and Journaling
Bonnie Thomas
ISBN 978 1 84905 842 1
eISBN 978 0 85700 417 8

Creative Coping Skills for Children
Emotional Support through Arts and Crafts Activities
Bonnie Thomas
Illustrated by Bonnie Thomas
ISBN 978 1 84310 921 1
eISBN 978 1 84642 954 5

More Creative Coping Skills for Children
Activities, Games, Stories, and Handouts
to Help Children Self-regulate
Bonnie Thomas
ISBN 978 1 78592 021 9
eISBN 978 1 78450 267 6

How to Get Kids Offline, Outdoors,
and Connecting with Nature
200+ Creative Activities to Encourage
Self-esteem, Mindfulness, and Wellbeing
Bonnie Thomas
ISBN 978 1 84905 968 8
eISBN 978 0 85700 853 4

CREATIVE COPING SKILLS FOR
TEENS AND TWEENS

ACTIVITIES FOR SELF CARE AND EMOTIONAL SUPPORT INCLUDING ART, YOGA, AND MINDFULNESS

Bonnie Thomas

Jessica Kingsley *Publishers*
London and Philadelphia

First published in 2019
by Jessica Kingsley Publishers
73 Collier Street
London N1 9BE, UK
and
400 Market Street, Suite 400
Philadelphia, PA 19106, USA

www.jkp.com

Copyright © Bonnie Thomas 2019

Library of Congress Cataloging in Publication Data
A CIP catalog record for this book is available from the Library of Congress

British Library Cataloguing in Publication Data
A CIP catalogue record for this book is available from the British Library

ISBN 978 1 78592 814 7
eISBN 978 1 78450 888 3

Printed and bound in the United States

The accompanying PDF can be downloaded from
www.jkp.com/voucher using the code GEAXONY.

Contents

Author's Note

This book is split up into five chapters, as follows:

1. Introduction

2. Self Care: How consistent self-care practices can positively impact your wellbeing.

3. Coping Skills: Coping strategies to use when stressors and uncomfortable feelings occur.

4. Creative Expression: Art and writing prompts that encourage you to explore who you are and what you've experienced, because the more you understand about yourself and your life experiences, the better able you are to take care of yourself and your needs.

5. For Parents: Pointers and support for parents of teens and tweens, because parents also need self care and support.

All pages marked with a ✳ can be photocopied and downloaded from www.jkp.com/voucher using the code GEAXONY for you to fill in alongside this book.

1

Introduction

• •

Over the past two decades I have worked with youth in many settings, but mainly in the field of counseling. During this time, teens and tweens have consistently presented with a multitude of challenges including shifts and changes within their peer groups; preparing for independence while needing—and many times wanting—parental guidance and support; testing boundaries and taking risks; planning for college and adulthood; keeping up with after-school activities, sports, and clubs; scrutinizing cultural norms to figure out where they fit in (and whether they even want to fit in); and ultimately taking care of themselves in a demanding world. Needless to say, this age group has a lot going on.

Part of my job as a counselor is to help clients learn new self-care and coping strategies to counter these stressors. I was inspired to write *Creative Coping Skills for Teens and Tweens* for this reason—to provide a resource that encapsulates various interventions for older youth that address self care, coping, self expression, and overall wellbeing.

Although the book is for counselors and providers like myself, it is also written for parents, as well as teens and tweens. I've written this book as if I am talking directly to the latter, and the reason for this is twofold:

1. This age group is savvy when it comes to real life issues. With social media and information technology, today's youth are much more aware of life challenges, adult topics, and more. Yet, as adults we often leave them out of opportunities to explore the issues they've been exposed to because we're either ignorant of their level of exposure to begin with, we might be uncomfortable addressing the issues ourselves, or perhaps we simply want to protect them as long a possible from these tougher topics. The bottom line is, we can't ignore the fact that

today's youth need to be included and pulled into the conversation about their own wellbeing. There are age-appropriate ways to do so, including the activities and discussion topics in this book.

2. For providers like myself who work with this age group, it makes for ease of sharing with clients of this age. For example, if I am meeting with a client who is struggling with a life-changing event, I can photocopy what I need, which is already reader-friendly for that client. I can go over it with the client, and send it home with them if helpful.

Note of caution: If you are a teen or tween reading this book on your own, please pay attention to any feelings that may arise from reading about some of the difficult feelings or life experiences mentioned. If at any time you feel unsure or uncomfortable while reading any part of this book, please talk to a trusted adult about it. If you feel unsafe at any time and a trusted adult is not available, please reach out to your local emergency or crisis support center. These emergency numbers change from state to state and country to country, so please take the time to write your personal emergency numbers here, for easy access:

_____

_____

COUNSELING ADOLESCENTS

Anna Atkinson, Transpersonal Arts Counselor

In my therapeutic experience, teens can be very good at keeping the door locked. "KEEP OUT," it says, scrawled on their psyche's entrance in black marker. The way in which we proceed to enter—with caution—is with three psychic knocks. In many well known myths and fairy tales, three is a common number: you get three wishes; three blind mice scurry about; three kings journey after a star; three little pigs hide from a wolf; and three witches cackle around a cauldron.

For me, three marks a process: a beginning, a middle, and an end. Teenagers are very much in the middle stage, sandwiched between the innocence of childhood and the stark demands of the adult world.

One way to examine this is to hold in mind the transformative nature cycle of the caterpillar, which is a three-stage process in nature—caterpillar, cocoon, and butterfly.

Stage 1: The Caterpillar

The first stage looks at the past—childhood. It considers biography and the thread that keeps someone bound in a certain story or family; the part that sometimes holds them back, keeping them stuck in possible unhealed trauma locked somewhere inside a latent toddler tantrum. The grip of their parents is still tight, and the old family pattern—if unhealed—can become unhealthy patterns or deep-seeded addictions later in adult life.

This is the stage where the resistance sits—the slammed doors, the not getting out of bed, the lethargy and the inertia. This is part of their identity—this is where the teen expresses a need to individuate. In this Caterpillar stage of counseling we honor their resistance and we sit with doors being slammed metaphorically in our face. We sit with patience and understanding that this is necessary for their growth. Their anger is very welcome. We are being tested if we are safe enough.

Stage 2: The Cocoon

This marks the point where the teen starts to engage. They tentatively start to trust the therapeutic process. They make emotive art in their locked bedrooms and bring their lyrical poems to sessions. They start to discuss sex and drugs and realize you are not going to judge them. They realize this is a safe space for them to sit and weave the cocoon with the threads of their life. At this stage the therapist has overcome the initial challenge of gaining the teenager's trust. This is the most delicate of the three stages and is where a therapist must observe the most proficient boundaries in order to protect their vulnerable client who is weaving a cocoon.

Stage 3: The Butterfly

This stage marks transcendence and change as the teenager prepares to fly off after a period of therapy. Something new is born within the psyche, marked by possibility and opportunity. This is where wings are found and independence becomes possible—the miracle moment, if you like.

This reflects the teenager's dream, their future, their legacy. During this part the therapist is allowing the teenage client their own autonomy, their own individual freedom to say, "This is me! This is the future I invite!" This last part of the process is rich, colorful, and free. There is an aspect of grief and loss during this last part, but the teen and therapist get to enact a good and healthy ending where separation and individuation take place naturally and safely.

These stages do not stand alone. They are part of a trinity, like a tripod that needs both gravity and levity to balance itself. As humans our deepest wounds are often in the gaps, the "in betweens." Finding the center during a well held journey gives us safety. It's the magic of the betwixt—the liminal space. It's a journey or reclamation, deep acknowledgement, and empowerment to step forth into adulthood.

2

Self Care

· ·

Self care is important because the better you take care of yourself, the better able you are to manage short- and long-term stress as well as illness, injury, and aging. Self care can also influence how your genes express themselves. This is important because ongoing unhealthy choices can have a negative impact, just as ongoing healthy choices can have a positive impact on your gene expression. This phenomenon and topic of gene expression is known as "epigenetics." If you're not familiar yet with epigenetics, you can read more about it in Dr. Aline Potvin's excerpt that follows, titled, "Nurturing your genetic blueprint." The overall point is that *self care plays a significant role in your health and wellbeing.*

Self care includes all of the things you do to take good care of your body and mind, such as eating healthy and getting exercise. The following topics are included in this chapter on self care:

- Eat nourishing foods and hydrate

- Sleep well

- Exercise and move your body

- Practice mindfulness

- Express gratitude

- Meditate

- Manage your time

- Play

- Embrace wonder

- Get motivated

- Appreciate your self

- Create healthy relationships

- Build community

NURTURING YOUR GENETIC BLUEPRINT ....

Dr. Aline Potvin, ND

"I feel like my brain never shuts down."

"Sometimes it's like my mind is on fire and I want to crawl out of my own skin."

"Most days I feel foggy and like I can't string my thoughts and words together quickly enough."

These are statements that many people can identify with, but it wasn't until quite recently that we understood that even emotional and physical experiences like this may be related to our genetic makeup. Typically, we inherit two copies of a gene (one from each parent) to create our unique code. There are approximately 23,000 genes found within our DNA, and they are packed around protein to make up the 46 chromosomes we inherit. The genes themselves are made up of a combination of four chemical base pairs, or nucleotides, linked together like the cars of a train. The basic role of DNA is to code for the production of proteins, including enzymes that run a lot of chemical reactions in our body. The function of these proteins and enzymes determine a lot about our physical selves, our ability to create energy, and our emotional/behavioral tendencies (Younique Genomics 2015).

Sometimes, spontaneously or due to an environmental trigger, there are changes to those base pairs in our DNA. A SNP (single nucleotide polymorphism) is created when one of those base pairs is set differently than its usual position. How does this relate to anxiety and overwhelm? Well, we have identified that some of these SNPs code for enzymes that may work slower or faster than usual. That means that having certain SNP copies can increase the possibility of heightened stress responses, difficulty relaxing, and anxiety or low mood (Lynch 2018, p.3).

We are still unsure as to why and how these changes in the genetic code came about. But it is clear that while many forms of genetic expression perhaps don't benefit us much now, at one time they did help us navigate our environment more effectively. We know that diabetes, for example, may have been a genetic advantage to people that lived in environments where food scarcity was common (Maurer 2014). My thought has always been that some of these SNP copies, that can contribute to increased anxiety and difficulty settling down, could have been very helpful at a time when vigilance was essential. That tasks like hunting, tracking, and keeping watch by the fire would have greatly benefited from some of the responses our bodies have to stressful situations. Many of the people I work with find this helpful to consider, but the reality is, we don't have to do those tasks anymore. So how can we support our bodies and nervous systems so that we can help our glorious blueprint work for us in everyday life?

What we are exploring now is the field of epigenetics, "epi-" meaning "outer," which is the study of how our genes express themselves in response to our environment. Many environmental factors affect our body's ability to influence the expression of these genes through a process called methylation. For methylation to work smoothly, it needs specific vitamins and minerals (Lynch 2018). So we know that diet and lifestyle specifically can have a lot of impact on how all our chemical reactions are running.

As I mentioned earlier, there are some commonly studied SNPs that may influence a lot about how our brain chemistry and emotional selves operate when we come up against challenges in our environment. For a lot of people it can be helpful to explore their genetic profile. Here are some examples of SNPs that can affect our mood:

- MTHFR: This gene codes for an enzyme that is key to the methylation process. When certain copies (SNPs) are present, the enzyme isn't able to function fully, which can influence over two hundred different processes in the body, including neurotransmitter production and recycling. People can respond in many different ways, but for some it can increase their anxiety levels or impact how their mood fluctuates throughout the day (Clinton 2017).

- COMT: The COMT gene codes for an enzyme that helps us break down adrenaline, which is a potent stress hormone. It is also responsible for recycling dopamine, a stimulating neurotransmitter. Having certain COMT SNPs may make these stimulating chemicals remain at higher levels for longer in the body, contributing to anxiety, difficulty sleeping, and other signs of being overstimulated (Lynch 2018).

- MAOA: This SNP copy can also make it difficult to calm down, sleep, and reduce fluctuations in mood because it codes for an enzyme that is key for processing the neurotransmitters serotonin and dopamine (Lynch 2018). It's not uncommon for people with this gene and the COMT SNP to be sensitive to caffeine.

Regardless of what SNP copies you have, how can you support your genes for their healthiest possible expression? The first step is to pin down some basics, including:

- Eat lots of leafy greens. Green vegetables contain a lot of naturally occurring folate, which is a key nutrient for methylation. They also have a lot of minerals, which can help our body break down adrenaline more effectively. Cooling salads and greens can help "cool our nervous system" if they are eaten regularly.

- Remove folic acid from your diet. This is really important when specific SNPs are present, like MTHFR, which I discussed earlier. Folic acid is a synthetic, inactive form of folate, and when it is abundant in the body, it can block the useful work of active forms of folate in the methylation process. It can make it difficult for our body to use active folate to help us break down stimulating neurotransmitters and maintain our energy. We find folic acid in a lot of foods made from flour, so if you're trying to reduce how much you take in, increasing fruit and vegetable-based snacks are a great way to do that.

- Be mindful of your digestion. A lot of gene expression is dependent on the nutrients we get from our diet, especially a variety of B vitamins and minerals. Even if you eat a diet really rich in fruits, vegetables, and healthy protein, it can be hard to benefit fully if you have difficulty absorbing those nutrients. Not only that, but a lot of how our nervous system works is directly connected to the enteric nervous system running the digestive tract. Frequent upset stomach, heartburn, and problems when using the bathroom tell us that our digestive tract may need additional support. It's really common for anxiety to contribute to stomach issues, but anxiety can also be a symptom of long-term digestive problems. It's always wise to talk to a healthcare provider you trust to help identify foods you might be sensitive to or other root causes for digestive concerns.

- Give yourself time to rest. Sometimes when we are anxious it can be hard to sleep, but it is important to make sure we are still getting enough rest. This is when we do most of our repairing, and it also allows important processes, like methylation, to work better (Clinton 2017).

Eat nourishing foods and hydrate

As a general rule, the healthier you eat, the healthier your body will be. The food and drink you put in your body has a major impact on your overall health including how well you manage stress. For example, have you ever spent a period of time (for some it could be a day, for others longer) when you ate mostly processed foods and drank soda or other drinks with a high sugar content? For some, this would result in feeling sluggish, moody, or having difficulty concentrating. A person who is feeling any of these is not going to feel in tip-top shape to solve problems, handle conflicts, or manage stressors when challenges arise.

Sweets and treats are wonderful for special occasions but moderation is key. Where possible, choose nutrient-dense foods that offer the vitamins and/or minerals your body needs. Unless you are allergic, try to incorporate these or other healthy foods into your diet when/if you can:

- Fruits

- Vegetables

- Hummus

- Babaganoush

- Bean dips

- Nut butters

- Seed butters

- Tahini

- Salsa

- Guacamole

- Meats, cheese, and eggs from grass-fed, humanely raised animals

- Nuts

- Roasted pumpkin seeds

- Dried coconut chips

- Dried meats/jerky

- Whole grain breads and crackers

- Whole grain pasta salad

- Popcorn

- Trail mix made with nuts and dried fruits

- Chia pudding

- Plain yogurt sweetened with local honey or fruit

- Roasted kale chips

- Roasted zucchini and/or carrot chips

- Vegetable fritters

- Roasted seaweed

- Tabbouleh

- Low sugar smoothies

- Low sugar nutrition bars/granola bars

I have also compiled a list of general suggestions for ways to increase your intake of healthier foods and stay hydrated in the handout titled "Nutrition and Hydration Tips." Highlight or checkmark any suggestions that you're willing or want to try on the list.

In addition, you can use the worksheet titled "My Action Plan: Nutrition and Hydration" to keep track of any nutritional goals you have as well list the healthy foods you enjoy. These are helpful to document for times when you need a reminder to stay focused on your nutrition goals.

*

Nutrition and Hydration Tips

Focus on eating the healthy foods you have access to and/or like to eat.

Keep a food journal to keep track of how your body reacts after you eat various foods and drink. If you see a pattern of not feeling well after eating or drinking something, remove that from your diet for a while to see if you feel better. Keep in mind that if you have slow digestion or delayed food allergies/sensitivities, you may not notice a reaction right away. This is why keeping a food journal is especially helpful. For example, you may notice that two to three days after eating certain foods that you feel fatigued and have trouble concentrating. If you keep a food journal for a period of time you can look for patterns more easily.

Drink plenty of water—your body is made mostly of water, and works best when you're hydrated.

Use a water bottle that you can fill up anywhere. Keep it in your backpack and bring it with you wherever you go. This will help you to stay hydrated.

Keep healthy grab-and-go snacks in your home for mornings when you feel rushed. Pack some in your backpack or purse for the ride or walk to school or work.

Set aside time at the beginning of the week to prepare and pack healthy snacks for the days ahead. Put the snacks in containers that are backpack-friendly and/or easy to grab "on the go."

If you feel like something is out of balance in your body, talk to your healthcare provider. Sometimes there are medical reasons for feeling "blah."

Supplement your diet with vitamins and minerals when needed. However, keep in mind that when you are eating healthy and getting plenty of rest, your body is less likely to need supplements and will be better able to create and convert the nutrients it needs on its own.

Abstain from using substances such as alcohol and illegal drugs; avoid vaping and smoking.

COPYRIGHT © BONNIE THOMAS 2019

My Action Plan: Nutrition and Hydration

This is what I'll work on to improve my nutrition and hydration:

_____

_____

_____

_____

_____

_____

_____

_____

Here is a reminder of the healthy foods I like:

_____

_____

_____

_____

_____

_____

Sleep well

Here are some interesting facts about sleep and why it is so important to self care:

> While you sleep, your brain is hard at work forming the pathways necessary for learning and creating memories and new insights. Without enough sleep, you can't focus and pay attention or respond quickly. A lack of sleep may even cause mood problems. Growing evidence shows that a chronic lack of sleep can also increase your risk of obesity, diabetes, cardiovascular disease, and infections. (NIH Medline Plus 2012)

> Studies also show that sleep deficiency alters activity in some parts of the brain. If you're sleep deficient, you may have trouble making decisions, solving problems, controlling your emotions and behavior, and coping with change. Sleep deficiency also has been linked to depression, suicide, and risk-taking behavior. (NHLBI n.d.)

Regardless of your age, sleep is critical to your physical and mental health. If you have trouble getting a good night's sleep, try a sleep visualization or one or more of the ideas on the handout titled, "Basic Tips for a Better Night's Sleep." You can also use the worksheet called, "My Action Plan: Better Sleep" to score the quality of your sleep, set a goal, and write down the actions you can take to improve your sleep. If you try these tips and still struggle getting a good night's rest, speak to a trusted adult and/or your healthcare provider.

On the opposite side of the issue, if you're sleeping a lot or "too much," then definitely speak to a trusted adult or doctor. Although sleep is healthy, too much may be a sign your body is out of balance and needs some support to get back to a healthier sleep pattern.

Basic Tips for a Better Night's Sleep

Avoid caffeine after noon—this includes tea, coffee, and dark chocolate.

Get plenty of exercise and/or time outdoors during the day.

When the sun goes down, switch the settings on your smartphone and computer for nighttime.

Make a to-do list for the next day—this is especially helpful if you're the kind of person who thinks of things you need to get done once you try to rest or relax.

Turn off electronics and screens at least one hour before you to go to bed.

Journal before you go to bed—get out anything that you need to say before you go to sleep.

Listen to a guided meditation or "binaural beats" to help you fall asleep.

Use a weighted blanket on your bed.

If you have a bathtub, take a bath before bed. Add a cup of Epsom salts or 2 drops of lavender essential oil to the water for added calming.

Talk to a parent and/or medical provider about whether supplements like tart cherry juice might help you sleep better.

Meditate or do gentle yoga before getting into bed.

Read in bed—choose a book that's engaging but not overstimulating. Read until you start to feel drowsy.

Use a sound machine to play relaxing tones or noises—e.g. the sound of ocean waves or rain.

Listen to relaxing music.

*

My Action Plan: Better Sleep

· ·

"Better sleep" includes getting enough hours of sleep per night, feeling rested when you wake up in the morning, and sleeping through the night without waking or disruption.

On a scale of 1–10 (1 being "horrible" and 10 being "amazing") how would you rate the quality of your sleep at this time? _____

What number on the scale would you like to aim for? _____

What can you do to improve your sleep? Refer to the "Basic Tips for a Better Night's Sleep" handout and write the ones you will try here:

_____

_____

_____

_____

_____

▶ VISUALIZATION FOR SLEEP

Visualization is when you use your imagination to mentally prepare for something. Some visualizations are more like guided meditations. Others are more goal-oriented. The goal of this visualization is to help you fall asleep more easily.

When you want to calm your body and mind for sleep, try this visualization:

- Think of a place where you feel relaxed and safe—it can be an imaginary place, a place you've been before, or a place you've always wanted to visit.

- Take a few moments to think about this place and where it is.

- Imagine yourself arriving at this place. What are the first clues you have arrived—is it something you smell, the change in landscape, or the way your body instantly feels calm? Or is it something else that cues you into knowing you've arrived here?

- Imagine yourself sitting or lying down in a comfortable, safe spot while you take in the scenery around you. What do you see, hear, smell, or feel in this relaxing and safe place?

- Give yourself positive messages such as, "I am safe here" and "I feel relaxed here."

- Remain with this visual until you drift off to sleep.

Even if you do not drift into sleep, your brain and body will quiet down and feel more restful. If you practice this same visualization each night, it will create a routine that your brain will soon recognize as a signal that it's time to quiet down and go to sleep. This means that the more you practice the same visualization, the easier and more successful it can be.

Exercise and move your body

There is no doubt that exercise and movement are good for bodies of all ages and stages of life. Each of us is different in what our bodies need for physical activity and in how we respond to exercise and movement. Some people prefer low-impact exercise, which may include yoga, swimming, or walking. For others, more intense activity may be desirable, such as running, working out at the gym, kickboxing, or skateboarding. Regardless of your activity level, find ways to get your body moving to the best of your ability. Exercise and movement are not just good for your body; they are also good for your mental health:

Regular aerobic exercise can reduce anxiety by making your brain's "fight or flight" system less reactive. When anxious people are exposed to physiological changes they fear, such as a rapid heartbeat, through regular aerobic exercise, they can develop a tolerance for such symptoms.

CREATIVE COPING SKILLS FOR TEENS AND TWEENS

Regular exercise such as cycling or gym-based aerobic, resistance, flexibility, and balance exercises can also reduce depressive symptoms. Exercise can be as effective as medication and psychotherapies. Regular exercise may boost mood by increasing a brain protein called BDNF that helps nerve fibers grow. (Pillay 2016)

▶ CREATIVE PHYSICAL ACTIVITY

People often think of exercise and movement in traditional terms, such as running, swimming, playing tennis, football, and so on. But there are many other options for getting movement in your life that are unique and fun. Consider the following ideas:

- Explore a local trail with friends.

- Go "letterboxing" or geocaching.

- Take fencing lessons.

- Use non-toxic glow-in-the-dark chalk to create grids and goals for night game play (e.g. Four Square, hopscotch).

- Create an obstacle course and see if a sibling or friend can beat your time completing it.

- Learn to play frisbee and/or learn frisbee tricks.

- Practice a cheerleading or dance routine with a friend.

- Sign up for a free gym trial—try the weightlifting equipment, a yoga class, exercise machines.

- Hula Hoop to your favorite music.

- Walk the entire length of a shopping mall.

- Rearrange your bedroom.

- Clean your room.

- Climb a tree.

- See how long you can Hula Hoop with your eyes closed.

- Learn a new kind of dance.

- Jump on a trampoline.

- Go bowling.

- Learn to ride a unicycle.

- Go trail riding on your bike.

- Try a themed yoga class such as "Yoga with Goats" or "Circus Yoga."

- Train for, and participate in, a themed race, e.g. a color run or a zombie run.

- Dance to your favorite music.

- Learn to juggle.

- Play laser tag.

- If you have a pet dog, take it on a walk or play an active game with it.

- Take a circus skills class.

- Get together with friends for a nighttime game of Manhunt or Flashlight Tag.

- Have a dance-off (dance contest) with your friends.

Keep in mind that some of these ideas may not require actual lessons—you may be able to learn new skills from friends or from online videos. Most importantly, use common sense and wear protective gear as needed.

▶ SHAKE AND STRETCH

- If you're feeling upset or if you need a moment to get re-focused, try "shaking it off"—literally shake and move your body. You can stomp your feet, dance, jump up and down, do jumping jacks, punch your fists in the air, or shake your limbs.

- When you're done shaking and moving all around, stop and take a few deep breaths. You can take a few forceful breaths or a few slow, calming breaths. Listen to what your body needs.

- Afterwards, stretch your arms, legs, back, and wherever else feels like it needs to stretch. Visualize the energy in your body reaching to the end of each finger and toe and flowing through you.

- Take another deep breath and bring your body back to a comfortable position.

YOGA: MOUNTAIN POSE AND COBRA POSE

Karla Helbert, LPC, E-RYT, C-IAYT[1]

Yoga teaches us to be present to what is, to accept where we are right now, in the present. It teaches us to adjust as we need to in order to be comfortable yet steady; to adapt and accommodate in order to maintain our comfortable steady posture, not only in asana, or on the yoga mat, but also in our daily lives.

You don't really need any special clothes or gear for yoga. You can use a yoga mat, but you can also do these on a clean floor or with a beach towel or thin blanket. Some of these you can just do wherever you happen to be, any time. Always be sure, though, for any standing poses, that whatever you are standing on will not slip or slide under your feet. I usually recommend stepping off the yoga mat for any standing and balance poses, because our balance is better on a firm, even surface.

Mountain pose, *tadasana* (*tada* = mountain)

This standing posture energizes the whole body. In it, you practice complete stillness and full activity of major muscle groups while opening your heart, focusing on breathing and strengthening your whole body. You can do this pose anywhere, any time.

When taking *tadasana*, bring the arms alongside the body first to feel balanced fully on both feet. Have the feet together or hip width apart, whatever feels steadier. Rock slightly from the balls of the feet to the heels, finding your balance. Allow the weight to be evenly distributed on both feet. Let the knees be straight, soft, not locked. The hips should be directly over the ankles. Lengthen the spine upward, roll the shoulders up, back and down, releasing them away from the ears. Extend the back of the neck upward, tucking the chin slightly. Leave the arms down, hands relaxed, fingers pointing toward the earth, or spread the palms wide. You may turn the palms toward the thighs or rotate the wrists so the palms face out or bring the hands together at the heart into a prayer position. Do what feels good to you. Feel as though you are aligning the energies of your body in the way that is right for you, right now. Feel your feet grounded into the earth, your feet like the base of a mountain, strong, steady, and rooted. Imagine your head reaching upward into the sky like a mountain peak. Feel your chest expand and open, receiving the rays of the sun. Breathe.

1   Author of *Yoga for Grief and Loss: Poses, Meditation, Devotion, Self-Reflection, Selfless Acts, Ritual* and *Finding Your Own Way to Grieve: A Creative Activity Workbook for Kids and Teens on the Autism Spectrum.*

Cobra pose, *bhujangasana* (*bhujang* = cobra)

Bhujangasana can help facilitate strength of self and a sense of openness toward others and the world. It is a posture of giving and receiving without judgment. The heart and the throat are open in this posture. If you have felt unable to fully communicate or express your thoughts and feelings, if your voice has been shut down or cut off, if your heart has felt closed or closely protected, emotional and energetic pain may be released in this posture. *Bhujangasana* cultivates courage and determination and helps ease worry. Physically, the posture helps to develop flexibility in the upper spine, stretches and strengthens the muscles of the neck and back, tones the abdominal organs, and increases circulation around the spine.

To come into cobra, lie on the belly, with the forehead to the mat, palms down, directly under the shoulders. The elbows should be close to the body. Gently, as if you are rolling a marble with your nose, stretch the chin forward, slowly raising the head, neck and chest, rolling the vertebrae back. Squeeze the shoulder blades together to increase the awareness there, noticing the energy in the chest and throat. Keep the neck extended, taking care not to compress the vertebrae. Lift the hands slightly to ensure that you are using the muscles of the back and not the arms. To release the posture, slowly bring the forehead back down to the mat.

Practice mindfulness

Mindfulness means bringing your attention to the present moment. It also involves accepting the ebb and flow of your feelings and thoughts.

Our minds are constantly observing and taking in information. We form thoughts based on these observations and then have feelings in reaction to the thoughts. Mindfulness is a way to accept that this is how our brains and bodies tend to flow, and that we can step aside and observe that flow without needing to respond to every thought and feeling. When a thought comes into your head you can acknowledge it and release it. When a feeling occurs, you can acknowledge it and release it also.

When you practice mindfulness on a regular basis it becomes a mindset that keeps you focused on the present moment rather than letting your imagination get stuck in a whirlwind of worst-case scenarios or strong emotions.

The following activities provide practice in mindfulness.

▶ OM POM POM

MATERIALS

Handful of small pom poms

Timer

DIRECTIONS

- Sit in a comfortable position with the timer nearby.

- Gather the pom poms into your lap.

- Take a few deep breaths to calm your body and thoughts.

- Set the timer for five minutes. During those five minutes keep your focus on the present moment. You can do this by focusing on your breathing; by tuning in to the smells, noises, and sensations you are experiencing at the moment; or by telling yourself, "I am here, now."

- If/when you notice that your thoughts have drifted or you have become distracted, move one of the pom poms from your lap to a spot in front of you. You can do this with your eyes closed.

- Go back to focusing on the present moment, and if you find you get distracted again, place another pom pom in front of you.

- When the five minutes is up and the timer goes off, notice how many pom poms are in front of you. It's okay if there are many—it's normal for our brains to get distracted. Each one of the pom poms represents an intention on your part to return to the present moment. If you practice this often enough, you may find that you have fewer and fewer pom poms in front of you as you become better at staying in the present moment.

▶ MINDFUL EATING

Eating can be a delightful way to practice mindfulness since most people enjoy food. Mindful eating means eating something one bite at a time, chewing your food fully before swallowing, and focusing on the sensations and tastes you receive from your food.

If you're the kind of person who frequently eats on the go, eats quickly, or can sit down with a box of cookies and eat them before you've even noticed, then mindful eating might be of benefit to you. It can be practiced at any time you're eating, whether it's a snack or a meal. The more you practice mindful eating the easier it becomes to apply the same mindset to other activities and moments.

▶ MINDFUL COMMUNICATION

Communication comes in many forms such as verbal communication, body language, and texting, to name a few. Regardless of the mode of communication, however, there are social norms and expectations that people ascribe to. For example, when people talk to each other it's usually expected that each person will be given opportunities to speak and be heard.

Some people have a harder time following communication norms—e.g. they might pick up their phone to answer a text when they are physically sitting next to someone who is talking to them; they might dominate a conversation and not pick up on cues that others are trying to join in with their own ideas or thoughts; or they might passively listen to what a person is saying, or not listen at all.

This is where mindful communication comes in. It means bringing your attention to your own words, tone of voice, and body language so that you are communicating and listening with intention. Mindful communication can be practiced in several ways depending on the moment. Here are some ways you can practice mindful communication:

VERBAL COMMUNICATION

- Listen to your tone of voice and observe your body language as you speak to others. Does your tone and body language match what you're trying to communicate? If you've ever heard someone yell, "Calm down, now!!" or if you've observed someone say, "I'm so sorry" while also laughing, then you know how confusing a message can become as a result of someone's tone of voice or body language.

- Pay attention to the words you speak. Are there certain words you use frequently? And if so, do you know why? Have the words become habit? Try to go an entire day without using one of your common words or phrases. Pay attention to the words you end up using instead; observe if other people communicate with you any differently, or if they even notice, and tune in to whether you feel more or less confident by removing these words from your vocabulary.

NON-VERBAL COMMUNICATION

- What non-verbal communication do you commonly use? Do you have a facial expression your parents or friends would say you use a lot? For instance, do you roll your eyes when you're annoyed? Spend a day paying attention to the things you communicate to others without using words—the things you "say" with your facial expressions, gestures, and body posturing instead.

Express gratitude

In terms of self care, gratitude is an inexpensive and low-risk means of boosting your mood and wellbeing. If you're feeling sad, depressed, or pessimistic, gratitude can help your brain recognize and feel more joy. Research shows that thinking grateful thoughts and expressing gratitude can make us feel happier (Harvard Health Publishing 2011). The following activities introduce ways to bring more gratitude into your life.

▶ GRATITUDE JOURNAL

Gratitude can be carried out in a variety of ways, but for the most powerful impact, try writing in a Gratitude Journal each day. Why? Each day that you write in a Gratitude Journal will reinforce the neurons in your brain to seek out things you feel gratitude for, and to feel it. The longer you practice this, the stronger those neurons will be, which means that gratitude will become more automatic. In return, you'll have more appreciation for yourself and others without much effort. Like most things in life, practice is what makes things easier.

MATERIALS

Plain and/or assorted papers

Stapler

Pencils, pens, and/or markers

DIRECTIONS

- You can make your own Gratitude Journal by folding some paper in half and stapling them. You can, of course, buy a blank journal to use, if you prefer, but it's good to know you always have the option to create your own.

- You can decorate your Gratitude Journal if you want. Some ideas for decorating include adding words and pictures from magazines of things you feel grateful for. Cut these images from magazine pages and glue them into your journal throughout the pages.

- Write at least three things each day that you are grateful for. Some days might be easier than others to come up with ideas, but here are some tips:

  - Look around your current environment and find something you appreciate about where you are right now—perhaps there's a beautiful pattern, shadow, or light where you are; maybe there is a shade of color that appeals to you; maybe you're wearing something that makes you feel comfortable or confident; or maybe there's something or someone within your reach that you appreciate.

- Think about things that you have access to on a regular basis that you appreciate, that others may take for granted. These include things such as clothing, shoes, shelter/a home, a meal, a person who cares about you, a pet, education, clean water, the right to speak up, etc.

- Consider the people who are in your life. Is there anyone in particular you are thankful for? If so, why?

- If you love a challenge, try this—think of someone you don't get along with. Name one thing (if there is one you can think of) that person has done that you appreciated.

- What foods are you grateful for?

- What things in nature are you grateful for? Are there certain animals that make you happy just knowing they are on this planet? Are there places in the natural world that make you feel awe, amazed, enchanted? Are you grateful for beaches, forests, mountains, or deserts?

- What books are you thankful for? Movies? TV shows?

- What art or music are you grateful for? Are there any art pieces that captivate your attention? What particular songs or lyrics make you feel thankful?

• Make sure to write in your Gratitude Journal each day.

*

Weekly Gratitude Journal
· ·

Each day write three things you feel gratitude for.

SUNDAY	1. 2. 3.
MONDAY	1. 2. 3.
TUESDAY	1. 2. 3.
WEDNESDAY	1. 2. 3.
THURSDAY	1. 2. 3.
FRIDAY	1. 2. 3.
SATURDAY	1. 2. 3.

▶ THANK YOU NOTES

I rarely meet with a client who is enthusiastic about writing Thank You Notes. Yes, they take time and organization, and writing them can feel like a chore. However, there are benefits to writing Thank You Notes that make it worth your time:

- Showing appreciation is good for you. It's a form of recognizing and expressing gratitude, which can boost your mood.

- The recipient will most likely appreciate the time and effort you put in to express your gratitude. It feels good to think of the recipient opening their Thank You Note and having that moment of feeling appreciated.

- It's good manners—manners make great impressions on others about who you are as a person. Good manners also give you an advantage in things like getting a job you want.

- It makes you more visible and memorable—people are more likely to remember you and your Thank You Note if/when there is another opportunity for them to do something for you.

You can buy Thank You Notes (or blank cards) or you can even make your own. Here is a sample Thank You Note:

Dear [fill in the blank],

How are you doing? I have been… [fill in what you've been doing lately such as school, work, spending time with friends, sports, etc.]. I wanted to take a moment to let you know how much I appreciate the [money, gift, time] you gave me. I especially enjoy [fill in a specific detail about your favorite part of the gift or how it impacted you in positive way]. Again, thank you! Be well.

Sincerely, [your name].

▶ RANDOM ACTS OF KINDNESS

Another means for practicing gratitude is to practice random acts of kindness. Completing random acts of kindness can have a positive effect on your wellbeing:

> This may be especially true for kids. Adolescents who identify their primary motive as helping others are three times happier than those who lack such altruistic motivation. Similarly, teens who are giving are also happier and more active, involved, excited, and engaged than their less engaged counterparts. Generous behavior reduces adolescent depression and suicide risk, and several studies have shown that teenagers who volunteer are less likely to fail a subject in school, get pregnant, or abuse substances. Teens who volunteer also tend to be more socially competent and have higher self-esteem. (Carter 2010)

> Like most medical antidepressants, kindness stimulates the production of serotonin. This feel-good chemical heals your wounds, calms you down, and makes you happy! (Random Acts of Kindness n.d.)

Many acts of kindness can be simple and free. Use the "Random Acts of Kindness and Gratitude" handout for suggested activities.

Random Acts of Kindness and Gratitude

If there is someone sitting alone at lunch, invite them to sit with you.

Open the door for someone.

When you notice someone doing a great job, tell them, "Great job!"

Offer to rake/clean up a neighbor's lawn.

Read a story to a younger sibling.

Leave a card or uplifting message for someone—e.g. on their locker, at their desk, on their door.

If it's snowy, offer to shovel a neighbor's walkway.

Make a special treat and deliver it to someone you appreciate.

Offer to go on a walk with someone (some people do not like to walk alone).

Compliment someone.

Tell someone how much you appreciate them.

Read out loud to a grandparent or elderly friend.

Gather the clothes/toys/books you no longer need and donate them.

Volunteer at a community event.

Being kind to the Earth: reuse, reduce, recycle.

Send an encouraging message to a friend or loved one.

If it's cold where you live, tie scarves and gloves/mittens to poles and benches with a note that says anyone who is in need of them can take them.

Fill small bags with basic items (e.g. snacks, a few dollars, toothpaste, toothbrush, deodorant, tissues, hand sanitizer, clean socks, etc.) and give them to homeless people.

Donate blood (if you're old enough).

If you live where it snows, shovel out a local fire hydrant so fire trucks have access to it if needed.

*

When someone does something kind for you say, "Thank you."

Take part in a fundraiser for a charitable cause.

Take part in an organized clean-up in the community—e.g. picking up litter in a local park or beach.

Learn basic sign language.

Donate clothing, books, or other items you no longer need.

Meditate

Meditation is one of those calming strategies that works beautifully for calming your mind and body. As a bonus, when you meditate on a regular basis (e.g. if you meditate a few times a week) it also helps to boost your immune system, decreases anxiety and depression, improves self regulation, and can increase your memory and focus too (Seppala 2013)!

Meditation can be a gentle routine that doesn't require special props or equipment. Give it a try!

▶ SIMPLE MEDITATION

- Find a comfortable spot where you will not be interrupted.

- Take a few deep, cleansing breaths. This will send a message to your body that you are ready to meditate.

- Close your eyes and give yourself a moment to settle in to the here and now.

- Choose something to bring your attention to, e.g. your breathing. A simple starting point is to inhale while you say to yourself, "breathe in calm" and then exhale, saying to yourself, "breathe out stress." You can also bring attention to feeling love in your heart while you say to yourself, "I feel love for myself and others" each time you complete a breath in and out.

- Stay with the meditation for as long as you can. It is common to lose focus and to find yourself lost in some other train of thought. When you notice your mind has wandered, bring yourself back to your focus point. The more you practice meditation, the less your mind will wander, but even experienced meditators experience mind wandering now and then!

- Check out the activity called "Om Pom Pom" which helps with meditation practice.

- You can further your practice by using smartphone apps for meditation, listening to guided meditations, or attending a meditation class.

▶ WALKING MEDITATION

A "walking meditation" might sound a bit silly, since most people think of meditation as sitting still with their eyes closed, but a walking meditation uses mindfulness and body awareness to help the mind focus and become still, and therefore, meditate. Some people enjoy a walking meditation in place of a sitting meditation because it provides movement and sensory input, which helps them quiet their minds better. Since everyone is different, you might want to try this walking meditation to see how it makes you feel. Try it at least once and then reflect on how your mind and body responded.

To practice a walking meditation:

- Choose a place to walk—it can be anywhere, as long as it is a safe area in which to walk.

- You may choose to walk with bare feet, but wearing shoes is also fine.

- Start walking. Notice your surroundings. What can you see around you? What do you smell? How does the air feel on your skin? What do you hear nearby versus in the distance?

- Next, start focusing on how your body is moving. Notice how your arms sway (or don't sway). Notice how your feet feel when they make contact with the ground. Notice the rhythm of your own body as it walks.

- As you walk, choose a sound, a movement, or a sensation to focus on. For example, continue to focus on just how your feet feel making contact with the earth, or just focus on the sound of birds singing.

- If at any time your mind starts to wander, bring your attention back to what you were focusing on.

- Practice this for at least 10 minutes if you can.

When your walking meditation is over, reflect on how your mind and body feel. Do either your mind or body feel quieter? Do you feel more in tune with your surroundings? Do you feel more focused? More relaxed? Or is there no change at all? Think it over while listening to your body and body cues. If there was any part of this walking meditation that felt calming to you, remember to try it again next time you want to quiet your mind.

Manage your time

Many cultures today embrace, and even glorify, being busy. There are certainly a number of youth who enjoy being busy and challenged—but that doesn't necessarily mean it's healthy. Being busy takes a toll on a person's wellbeing, even when they enjoy that level of activity.

In the past few years I've observed an epidemic of sorts: patient after patient suffering from the same condition. The symptoms of this condition include fatigue, irritability, insomnia, anxiety, headaches, heartburn, bowel disturbances, back pain, and weight gain. There are no blood tests or X-rays diagnostic of this condition, and yet it's easy to recognize. The condition is excessive busy-ness (Koven 2013).

Time management is an important skill to learn because it helps you to schedule your time more effectively, which can help reduce stress levels. To practice time management, let's first look at how you spend your time.

▶ MAP YOUR TIME

This is where you create a visual of how you spend your time. This is informative because it shows you if you're using "too much" or "too little" time doing certain activities. For example, if you don't see any time in your map dedicated to self care, you may want to adjust your schedule to include it.

MATERIALS

Paper

Pencil

Optional: Two copies of the "Map Your Time" worksheet

DIRECTIONS

- If you have access to a photocopier, you can make two copies of the "Map Your Time" worksheet OR draw two timelines with 24 sections—each section represents an hour of the day.

- Label the hours on each timeline, starting and ending at midnight.

- Choose a day of the week that is typically your busiest day. Label your timeline with that day of the week.

- Fill in how you typically spend your time on this day of the week. For example, mark down what time you wake up, the time you spend getting ready for the day, the time you eat meals, the hours you attend school (or work), the time spent at any after-school activities, homework, and what time you tend to go to sleep.

- Next, choose a day of the week that tends to be the quietest for you and repeat the steps above. This will give you two timelines to compare—a typical busy day for you versus a typical quiet day.

REFLECTION

- Look over your two timelines. What do you notice, if anything, about these two different days?

- Do you feel any differently looking at one day versus the other?

- If you could change anything about either day, would you?

- Do you have at least 15 minutes each day to do something for stress management or self care?

If you see any places in your timeline where you notice it looks or feels overwhelming, plan ahead and think about what you can do to counteract or reduce some of that activity and/or stress. Mapping your time means looking at how you spend your time, but also finding places to squeeze in self care, especially on busy days. Here are some examples of ways to provide proactive or quick self care:

- Shut your eyes and take a few deep breaths. Tune out any of the busy-ness around you, and just shut down for a minute to recharge your senses.

- Take three deep belly breaths.

- Spend an extra minute washing your hands—feel the warmth or coolness of the water as you massage any tired muscles in your hands and fingers.

- Stretch your arms, legs, neck, and/or back.

- Cup your hands over your eyes for a few moments. Tell yourself something positive or remind yourself of something you are looking forward to.

Map Your Time

Date: _____

Fill each line with activities you did during that hour, e.g. eat, sleep, homework, school, work, go online, sports, video games, etc.

12 midnight	
1 am	
2 am	
3 am	
4 am	
5 am	
6 am	
7 am	
8 am	
9 am	
10 am	
11 am	
12 noon	
1 pm	
2 pm	
3 pm	
4 pm	
5 pm	
6 pm	
7 pm	
8 pm	
9 pm	
10 pm	
11 pm	

▶ CREATE FREE TIME

Take a few moments to write down or think about the following. If there were no restrictions on how you spend your time, how would you spend it? How would you spend your "free time"?

Pretend for a moment that you have no obligations such as work, school, chores, sports, clubs, and so on, and you can spend every minute as you please. Brainstorm all the activities you would do simply because you enjoy them. Then look over your list.

REFLECTION

- Do you feel like you get enough of these activities in your life in general? If yes, what does that feel like to you? And if no, what does that feel like to you?

- Put a mark next to the activities that require money or transportation.

- Look at the activities that do not require money or transportation—these are more likely to be accessible to you or in your control. How can you add more of these activities into your life?

Free time is important for us as it allows time to unwind, relax, and rest. It also allows time for us to play, be creative, and feel unconstrained. If you do not have any (or enough) free time in your schedule, then talk to a parent or trusted adult to see what, if any, changes can be made.

▶ PLAN AHEAD

If you plan ahead you can schedule time for what needs to get done as well as what you want to get done. There are different strategies for planning ahead such as writing "to-do" lists (see the worksheets "To-Do Lists" and "Time Management"). Here are some tips on using "to-do" lists:

- Each evening write a note or "to-do" list of what you need to get done the next day.

- Be specific and realistic about tasks you write on your "to-do" list. For example, if you write down "Write a five-page paper for English," you might feel overwhelmed just looking at it. However, if you break down large tasks into smaller tasks, it will make it easier to accomplish goals. You could write instead:

  — Create an outline for English paper.

  — Write rough draft for English paper.

  — Create title for English paper.

  — Review and edit rough draft for English paper.

- Keep any "to-do" lists in a place where you can access them easily.

- Mark off tasks as you complete them.

Other tips for organizing your time:

- Use an app on your smartphone that helps you organize your time.

- Use an organizer or appointment book where you can keep track of all of your responsibilities and deadlines.

- Schedule self care and free time for yourself.

- If there are certain times of the week, month, or year that are particularly tough for you, make sure you schedule in extra self care prior to, and during, that time.

*

To-Do Lists

. . . .

Cut out the following "To-Do Lists" and use them as needed to list what you need to get done.

My To-Do List	My To-Do List
My To-Do List	My To-Do List

Time Management

· ·

Break goals and assignments down into smaller, more manageable steps.

My goal/assignment is:

_____

_____

_____

This is how I can break it down into smaller, more manageable steps:

1. _____

2. _____

3. _____

4. _____

5. _____

6. _____

7. _____

8. _____

*

Weekly planner for week of: _____

Day of the week	Morning	Afternoon	Evening
Sunday			
Monday			
Tuesday			
Wednesday			
Thursday			
Friday			
Saturday			

Play

Regardless of your age, play is important to your mental and physical health:

> Researchers have documented a rise in mental health problems—such as anxiety and depression—among young people that has paralleled a decline in children's opportunities to play. And while play has gotten deserved press in recent months for its role in fostering crucial social-emotional and cognitive skills and cultivating creativity and imagination in the early childhood years, a critical group has been largely left out of these important conversations. Adolescents, too—not to mention adults, as shown through Google's efforts—need time to play, and they need time to play in school. (Conklin 2015)

> Play often leads to laughter, which has been linked to decreased stress and inflammation and may improve vascular health. 'Your blood pressure goes down,' he said. 'You release dopamine.' (Chillag 2017, quoting Dr. Bowen White 2017).

Obviously, "play" looks different depending on your age and interests, but the following activities provide playful ideas to try alone or with friends.

▶ SOLO PLAY

The list of activities that follow can be done on your own, by yourself; they can also be done with others:

- Learn to catch popcorn in your mouth.

- Make banana art: Do not peel the banana. Use a disinfected needle to poke holes in the peel. Create a pattern, picture, or spell out words with the tiny holes. After a bit of time, the holes will turn brown and then reveal what you created.

- Decorate cookies or cupcakes with frosting, candies, and/or sprinkles.

- Hide positive and uplifting messages in places where people will find them.

- Watch a comedy.

- Make your own fortunes for fortune cookies—remove fortunes from store-bought fortune cookies (tweezers can help with this) and replace the fortunes with the ones you made.

- Create a selfie scavenger hunt for your friends (see "Create an adventurous scavenger hunt" below).

- Play with a pet.

- Color or do puzzles in an activity book.

- Climb a tree.

- Learn a magic trick.

- Flip through flip books.

- Make a blanket fort.

- Build something fun (e.g. a spoon catapult, a marshmallow shooter).

- Create a project from a craft book (e.g. a gum wrapper chain).

- Skip stones in a pond, lake, or ocean.

- Choose an object like a bottle cap, paper clip, penny, or small figurine and start hiding them where friends or family members will find them. They will wonder where they keep coming from.

- Learn to bake or cook something. Try a new recipe.

- Visit your local library and see what new materials you can borrow—books, movies, games, puzzles, and more.

- Send snail mail (write a letter) to a friend or family member.

- Learn to spin a basketball on your finger.

- Create a time capsule. A time capsule is a container that is filled with objects from a specific year or time period that is then buried for you or for others to find in the future.

- Secretly clean an area of your home, and then deny you had anything to do with it.

- Watch home movies from when you were little, or look through old photographs.

- Paint your nails in a new design or color.

- If you have snow, make a fun snow sculpture—e.g. build a snow person that holds bird seed for the birds or build an upside-down snowperson.

- Write a letter to your future self (see "Letter to Your Younger Self" later).

- Research and practice new ways to whistle, e.g. with a blade of grass, your fingers or an acorn cap.

- Apply temporary tattoos to boiled eggs—apply to the outer shell once the eggs are cooled.

- Start a blog about something you're interested in.

- Try different "slime" recipes such as glitter slime or glow in the dark slime.

- Make your own spa beauty products such as sugar scrubs, bath bombs, or facial masks, and have a spa night.

- Make a friendship bracelet.

- Create a tabletop mini golf.

- Make a black light craft such as "glow bubbles" (these are bubbles that glow under a black light). You can search online for "glow in the dark crafts" or "black light crafts."

- Build a fairy house or gnome home where a child will discover it.

- Go puddle jumping.

- Make a "card house" with playing cards.

- Play with clay or Play-Doh.

- Make and fly paper airplanes.

- Read your favorite childhood books.

- Try a new form or origami, such as electric origami or money origami.

- Create a "toast sampler"—cut toast into squares, triangles, or others shapes, and use various spreads for the toast such as hummus, butter, nut butter, seed butter, jam/jelly, cream cheese, herbed butter, cheese spread, avocado, apple butter, and so on.

▶ PLAYFUL ACTIVITIES WITH FRIENDS

Almost any activity with friends can be fun simply because you're doing so with people you enjoy being with. Here are some playful activities that work well with friends:

- Visit a local haunt (but do not trespass—take pictures from afar if needed).

- Challenge a friend to a thumb wrestling match.

- Sing karaoke.

- Play board games.

- Visit an amusement park.

- Go wading at a local swimming hole.

- Participate in "urban gaming" or "location-based games." These games typically require a mobile device and/or a GPS that allows you to game with others on location. Make sure to connect with reputable game organizers and bring someone with you.

▶ HAVE A RECYCLED FASHION SHOW

Challenge your friends to a fashion show where all of the clothing and accessories are created with 100 percent recycled materials. Set a deadline for the fashion show that allows reasonable time for everyone to complete their project. On the day of the event clear a space for a "stage" area. Designate a room where people can change in and out of their outfits. Play music and take turns showing off your fashion creations with each other. If you like, create various awards such as "Most creative use of soda can tabs."

▶ CREATE AN ADVENTUROUS SCAVENGER HUNT

When I was in high school my best friend and I hosted an island-wide scavenger hunt where we lived. Each team of players had to collect certain items at various locations and complete challenges along the way. The goal of the scavenger hunt was to experience a unique and fun adventure with friends.

You can also plan an adventurous scavenger hunt for your friends. Once you decide on a date, who is participating, and where it will take place, the next step is to brainstorm actions and items to be "collected" based on your location. Think about all the places in your neighborhood or town that a group of you and your friends could safely and easily go to, and incorporate those places into your scavenger hunt. Here are some ideas to get you started:

ADVENTUROUS SCAVENGER HUNT LOCATION: YOUR TOWN

- Take a group selfie in front of a local landmark.

- Document an act of kindness, e.g. "here's a photo of us putting change in someone's parking meter."

- Bring back these items: a business card from a local establishment; an autograph from the local librarian; a receipt; a list someone left behind in a basket or cart at the grocery store.

- Take a group selfie from two different historical sites in town.

ADVENTUROUS SCAVENGER HUNT LOCATION: THE SHOPPING MALL

- Bring back the following: a free sample of something; a napkin; a token or ticket from the arcade; a pamphlet or brochure; a fortune from a fortune cookie.

- These five photos must be taken: someone in the group trying on a formal gown; someone in the group with a puppet on their hand; a group selfie taken in front of the carousel or play area; someone in the group reading a book about something they're truly interested in; and a group selfie of everyone wearing feather boas or sunglasses.

ADVENTUROUS SCAVENGER HUNT LOCATION: OUTDOORS/NATURE

- Create a small piece of land art that does not involve trespassing, littering, or breaking any ordinances. Take a photo of it and then put the items back where you found them.

- Bring back the following objects—something green; a bottle cap; a rock shaped like a piece of food; a flat rock; a seed pod; a Y-shaped stick; something with a stem; a curious object; a trail map; a discarded/found item.

- Bring back photos of the following: a tree that looks like fun to climb; a selfie in front of a beautiful spot; an animal/insect; a plant with thorns; a flower; something white; a footprint.

Make sure to get a group photo at the end of the scavenger hunt for posterity.

▶ ORGANIZE A THEMED GATHERING

Themed gatherings mean hanging out with friends and planning food or activities for that event based on a specific theme. For example, if your friends are going to watch a favorite TV series or movie, dress up as the characters, have a trivia competition about it, and/or only eat foods that are eaten in the story. Here are other themes to consider:

- Coordinate a gathering where you and your friends make your favorite recipes and eat a meal together.

- Plan a movie marathon where all the movies have a similar theme, e.g. a horror movie marathon.

- Have a get-together based on an era—e.g. an 80s gathering. Dress in 80s fashion, eat food that was popular in the 80s, watch an 80s show, or do a craft from that era (e.g. friendship pins or braided ribbon barrettes).

- Have a game night where all the snacks are based on the games you are playing.

- Have a pajama-themed gathering—everyone comes in their pajamas and slippers.

What other themes would you and your friends enjoy?

▶ HAVE A RAINBOW POWDER FIGHT

If you've celebrated Holi (Festival of Colors) or been to a "Color Run," then perhaps you've experienced the fun of getting covered in brightly colored powders. These powders are not just for festivals and large events, however—you can purchase them for your own celebration, or even make your own.

If you want to make your own "Holi powder" or "color powder," search online for a recipe that best fits your budget and needs. For example, some of the recipes use cornstarch, which is better for those with gluten intolerance; other recipes call for flour; some use liquid pigment (food coloring); and others use powdered pigment.

Make sure to wear clothing you don't mind getting stained when making or using the powders.

Once you have your powders, choose a location where there's plenty of space (you don't want powder getting on passersby or property). Hand out a different color to each friend, then count to three and throw the powder at each other, aiming low so as to avoid each other's eyes.

Wash your clothes soon after the fun.

▶ GO ON A NIGHTTIME ADVENTURE

If you live in an area where it's safe to do so, spending time outdoors at night can feel like a magical adventure. Get together with one or more of your friends for one of these nighttime experiences:

- Take a walk on the night of a full moon.

- Pitch a tent in your backyard and spend some or all of the night out there.

- Walk around the city where it's safe to do so.

- If owls live in your area, go on an owl walk where they're known to reside. Listen for their calls in the dark.

- If you live in a rural area, look for bioluminescent fungi in wooded areas.

- If fireflies inhabit your neighborhood, go for a firefly walk.

- Ask a parent or chaperone to take you on a night drive to look at the city skyline, a sunset, or holiday light displays.

- Have a night picnic on your back steps or in the backyard.

- Get together with your friends to howl at the moon.

- On the date of the next meteor shower, gather at a location where there's minimal light pollution and observe the meteors.

- Go to a drive-in movie.

Embrace wonder

A recent trend in the modern world is glorifying "busy-ness"—being busy. However, as life becomes more frenzied and hectic, people become more stressed, overworked, and exhausted. Human beings need a balanced life—one that allows for time to unwind, relax, play, explore, and use their imagination. This is where wonder comes in as a self-care strategy—it's an antidote to the intensity and drive of modern-day life.

Wonder is a feeling often associated with fairy tales, magic, imagination, and awe. The following activities show you how to invite more wonder into your life.

▶ CREATE A SECRET HIDEAWAY

What do the following places share in common?

Forts, tree houses, fields, closets, caves, gardens, tents, trees, forests, tipis, riversides, alleyways, under the bed, attics, stairwells, cardboard boxes, blanket forts…

Answer: They've all been reborn as secret hideaways.

Childhood can be forever changed by the spaces children call "secret hideaways." Whether they exist for five minutes or five years, "secret hideaways" become places where kingdoms rise and fall in the blink of an eye; power is felt; memories are made; sleep is voluntary; intuition is palpable; dreams are put into motion; promises are made; prayers are said; imaginary worlds come to life; friendships are nurtured; songs are sung; war and peace are waged; tears are shed; stories come to life; things are buried; rites of passage are celebrated; secrets are told; quiet is honored; muses are played with; art is created; giggles become unstoppable; creativity blooms; food becomes tastier; rituals are honored; music is savored; books are devoured; spirits are spoken to; secret languages are created; love is invited; and play is honored.

Regardless of your age it's gratifying to have a space where you can go—where the world disappears behind you and you can melt into the moment, whatever that moment needs to be. Yes, this is ideal, and not everyone can have such a space, but if at all possible, consider creating one for yourself.

When creating a secret hideaway, simpler is better. Designate a small space, such as a corner of a room or a closet, and decorate that area with items that feel enchanting, magical, or inspiring to you. You can include books you've been wanting to read, a journal to write in, string lights, a meditation pillow or crystal, things that make you laugh or smile, a collection of things that make you feel joyful, a stuffed animal, a battery-operated candle or lantern, and so on.

If space is limited (or even non-existent), try a portable or temporary option: Create a blanket fort—these are as fun for tweens and teens as they are for kids; put a few items in a backpack or bag that you can bring anywhere to create an "instant" hideaway, and include a blanket to hang up or sit on and any small items that provide comfort and inspiration; or if there is no space at all, make a sketch, collage, or motivation board of what you want your space to look like when you have the means to create it.

▶ CREATE A WONDER JOURNAL

A Wonder Journal is a sketchbook that is transformed into a collection of photos, lists, and pictures that instill wonder in you. It's a whimsical treasure to create as a reminder of all the mysteries and wonder that captivate your imagination. When life gets complicated, messy, or even boring, look through your Wonder Journal for a distraction and a mood lifter.

MATERIALS

Sketchbook with blank pages

Writing utensils—pens, pencils, colored pencils

Glue

Scissors

Internet access and a printer (optional)

Collected and trimmed images from magazines and other printed material

DIRECTIONS

List, describe, illustrate, or provide photos of any/all of the following that interest you:

- animals that have saved humans

- "ghost towns" such as Bodie, California, and other abandoned locations

- extraordinary acts of kindness

- secret societies

- people with unusually high IQs and/or those with extraordinary gifts and talents

- stories about coincidence, serendipity, and extremely good luck

- paranormal or unexplained activity, e.g. precognition, ghosts, miracles, etc.

- nature and natural phenomena that amaze you, e.g. bioluminescent plants and animals, the Northern Lights, tsunamis, etc.

- unlikely friendships between different species of animals

- people who've survived unbelievable odds

- unsolved mathematical equations

- crop circles

- secret codes and languages

- awe-inspiring works of art, music, engineering, design, or innovation

- movies, books, and other media that have inspired you

- unsolved mysteries

- riddles

- anything else that makes you curious and full of wonder.

Glue these items and/or list them on the pages of your Wonder Journal.

Get motivated

What goals do you want to achieve in your lifetime? What do you want to experience? What memories do you hope to create for yourself?

When you identify your hopes, dreams, and goals, you remind yourself of the rewards you want in life. Motivation is what drives you to do the work needed to get those rewards. When you feel overwhelmed, unappreciated, invisible, or just down, it's nice to have motivators to keep you focused on what's most important to you.

The following activities highlight various ways to document your hopes and dreams so you can refer to them as needed to help you stay motivated, especially during tough times.

▶ MOTIVATION BOARDS

A Motivation Board is a large collage of words, quotes, and images that represent your hopes and dreams. Your board can be hung on a wall to remind you of all the adventures and life goals you want to experience.

MATERIALS

Poster board

Collage materials—photos, magazines, and other printed materials

Decoupage glue or white glue

Paint brush

Markers

Pen

Scissors

DIRECTIONS

- Start a list of what you hope and dream for—include the places you want to travel to, the career you want, pets you'd like, goals you want to accomplish, and experiences you desire.

- Add any quotes, words, or names of people that motivate and inspire you to the list as well.

- Look through your collage materials and search for images and words that represent anything on your list.

- If you don't find an image for something you listed, draw it or write it down and then cut it out. If you have access to a computer and printer, you can print out a specific image as needed.

- Arrange the words and images on the poster board. Get an idea of where you'd like the pictures and words to go.

- Glue the words and images from your collage collection onto the poster board.

- Decorate any empty spaces and the border around the poster.

- Hang your Motivation Board in a place where you'll be able to see it often.

▶ LIFETIME WISH LIST

A Lifetime Wish List is a checklist of things you want to experience in your lifetime. It's a motivational document because it reminds you of what your heart and soul desires—from the small things to the bigger things. Small things are goals such as, "I want to try sour jellybeans." Bigger things are goals such as, "I want to graduate from high school/college" or "I want to step foot in all seven continents." Whenever you accomplish something on your Lifetime Wish List, put a checkmark next to it. You can add items to your Wish List for as long as you have it.

▶ ROLE MODELS

Role Models are people who inspire you. They are people who motivate you to meet your goals and do your best. They can be alive or dead, a person you know, or a famous person.

For this activity you will discover new Role Models for yourself. This list can be convenient in times when you need a reminder of who you aspire to be or what you want to achieve, especially when you're feeling defeated or feel like giving up.

MATERIALS

Internet access

Pen and paper

DIRECTIONS

The goal is to find a Role Model in each of these categories:

- in a career you want

- with similar passions or interests as you

- with similar life experiences or life challenges as you.

Use your internet browser to search for famous people and role models who fit the categories above. A search in each category might look like:

Famous farmers; celebrated architects; role models in the fashion industry; famous chess champions; famous manga artists; role models in basketball; famous people with disabilities; unpopular celebrities; famous people who were adopted; famous people with bipolar disorder

Read up on the various people who come up in your searches. It can be inspiring to read or hear their stories and learn how they managed to be successful in achieving their aims. See if you can find one person in each category that you admire or respect, and then add them to your list (use the worksheet "My Role Models"). Obviously if you find more than one Role Model in each category, that's great! Add as many as you wish. Maybe you'll end up on someone's Role Model list someday too!

*

My Role Models

. . . .

List names and/or attach photos of your role models below. Write at least one thing you admire about each one or why you chose them as a role model.

_____

_____

_____

_____

_____

_____

_____

_____

_____

_____

Appreciate yourself

Appreciating yourself means accepting and honoring all of you—even the parts you perceive as imperfections.

Many teens and tweens (adults, too) struggle with appreciating themselves. Many people feel they should look and act a certain way based on what they see in social media, magazines, television, movies, and so on. It can be tough to honor and love your body, especially if you live in a culture where certain sizes, skin color, behaviors, and appearances are portrayed favoring one over another.

Appreciating and honoring yourself takes dedication and work, but there are ways to go about changing your perception of yourself in a more loving way. This includes using daily affirmations, reframing how you view your body and self, as well as using self expression to honor your voice, your life story, and you.

▶ AFFIRMATIONS

Many people give themselves negative messages and negative self talk, especially about their appearance and self worth. Examples of negative self talk include, "I'm so stupid—why did I do that?!," "I look ugly," or "No one likes me." As I'm sure you can imagine (or may even know from first-hand experience), negative self talk is not helpful, and in some ways it can be harmful.

Affirmations, however, are the opposite. Affirmations are messages you intentionally tell yourself that are words of encouragement and support. Affirmations can help you change the way you think about yourself due to a phenomenon called "neuroplasticity"—you can change the way your brain thinks by practicing new thoughts—such as telling yourself positive messages instead of negative ones. One way to help fight off negative self talk is to practice affirmations. Set aside time each day to repeat positive messages to yourself, such as:

I am lovable.

I'm doing my best.

I can do this.

I will be kind to myself today.

I am worthy of love and respect.

I love my uniqueness.

Today I embrace my imperfections.

I'm courageous—I can do this.

*

Affirmations

My positive thought/affirmation for today is:

_____

_____

_____

_____

▶ | THE STORY FROM THESE BONES

"The Story from These Bones" is an activity where you reflect on—and write about—your life experiences, but you list your life experiences specific to one part of your body. For example, if your hands could tell your life story, your hands might "remember" the people you've enjoyed holding hands with, a beautiful picture you've drawn, or a time you unwrapped a favorite gift.

If you have trouble appreciating your body as a whole (e.g. if you ever say "I hate my body") this activity may help you view your body in a more positive way. When you narrow your focus and reflect on just one part of your body, it's easier to have appreciation for the experiences that part of your body has gifted you. Repeat this exercise for as many body areas as you want.

DIRECTIONS

Choose a body "area" from the list:

feet	lungs	mouth
knees	hands	voice
stomach	eyes	spirit
heart	ears	

Think about what that part of your body has experienced in your lifetime. Specifically, brainstorm all the positive memories that part of your body has experienced.

Here are some guided questions to get you started.

Feet

- Where have these feet walked barefoot?

- What bodies of water have these feet stood in?

- Where have these feet travelled?

- Are there certain places you've stood that were memorable or meaningful?

- When have your feet helped you to run away from something?

- When have your feet stayed in place when you were standing your ground?

- What dances have your feet experienced?

- Have you ever chased someone—or been chased—for fun?

- Have you ever ridden a bicycle?

Here are some feet-related verbs to think about using: walked, stomped, walked on tip toe, stood on tip toe, limped, kicked, ran, chased, sleepwalked, peddled, danced, sprinted, scurried, bolted, gave chase, resisted, held firm, arrived at, escaped, survived.

Knees

- What accomplishments and projects have your knees played a role in? For example, have you ever worked in a garden, created an art project, or done another activity in which you spent time kneeling?

- What have your knees helped you ascend, descend, or climb? For example, have your knees helped you climb any trees, mountains, or ladders?

- Have your knees helped you balance while doing any agility activities? For example, have they helped you while balance walking across a log, ice-skating, or dancing?

- Have you ever picked up something really heavy where you used your knees to help you hold up the weight?

Knee-related verbs: knelt, straddled, ascended, descended, balanced, bent, beared the weight of.

Stomach

- Your stomach has ingested a variety of foods that are connected to many "firsts"— your first bite of solid food, your first birthday cake, your first time trying a foreign food, etc. What stories would your stomach tell about some of these "food firsts"?

- What stories would your stomach tell about moments when you got to eat your most favorite foods?

- Have you ever had a small pet curl up and fall asleep on your stomach?

- Have you ever had a "belly laugh"?

- Have you ever experienced intuition, or what others call "a gut feeling"? Has a gut feeling ever saved you from danger?

- What positive experiences have you had lying on your belly? For example, lying on the beach, lying in the grass, body surfing, or sledding.

Stomach-related verbs: digested, vomited, "had butterflies," intuited.

Heart

- When has your heart felt joy?

- Who do you love with "all your heart"?

- What have you longed and wished for—what has been your "heart's desire"?

- When have you "found it in your heart" to forgive someone or do something kind for someone?

- Has anyone ever done or said something so sweet, loving, or kind that it "melted your heart"?

- Describe a time your heart was "in the right place" and you made a good choice.

- What makes your heart race in a good way?

Heart-related verbs: felt loved, pumped, burst, skipped a beat/did a flip, swelled with joy.

Lungs

- Where have you breathed the freshest, cleanest air?

- Have you ever played a game in the water, or swam underwater, where you had to hold your breath?

- When have you been out of breath, for example, climbing a mountain, running a race, playing tag, laughing?

- What is something you have shouted or sang "at the top of your lungs"?

- Have you ever blown out birthday candles?

Lung-related verbs: breathed, inhaled, exhaled.

Hands

- What have you hung from—or onto—before? For example, swings, ropes, monkey bars, tree branches, rocks/rock climbing, etc.

- Whom have you held hands with?

- Whose hand is your favorite to hold?

- Have you ever made a "pinky swear" or shook hands on a promise?

- Have you driven a car before? If so, how did it feel to start and steer a car for the first time?

- When were times you got your hands messy for fun? For example, making mud pies or finger painting.

- What things have you created or written that you feel proud of?

- What moments in your life have your crossed your fingers for good luck?

- Have you ever visited a palm reader or studied your own palm? If so, what did you learn?

- Have you ever had a manicure?

- Have you had henna painted on your hands before?

- Do you know sign language?

- Have you ever had a secret hand signal or handshake with a best friend?

Hand-related verbs: held, grasped, pinched, grabbed, patted, pulled, pushed, punched, pointed, signed, motioned, signaled, squeezed, crafted, drew, painted, wrote, sculpted, scribbled, drafted, shaped, wiped tears, prayed, reached for.

Eyes

- What are some extraordinary things your eyes have seen?

- Have you ever had a staring contest?

- What color are your eyes?

- Has anyone complimented your eyes before? If so, what did they say?

- What details, colors, and patterns are your eyes attracted to? What catches your attention?

- What movies have you seen that had visuals you enjoyed?

- What beautiful moments have brought you to tears?

Eye-related verbs: saw, blinked, ignored, observed, spied, watched, stared, cried, winked, glanced, rolled, glared, scrutinized, witnessed.

Ears

- Whose voice is most soothing to you?

- What music or noise calms you?

- What music or noise makes you feel joy?

- What sounds remind you of positive moments about being a kid?

- What are your favorite sounds?

- Do you like to be read to? Do you have memories of being read to as a kid?

- What does your home sound like during the day? And during the night?

- What sounds might people hear in your yard or neighborhood?

- Describe a time when you heard a weird noise and you figured out where it was coming from.

- Are your ears pierced?

- Have you ever ignored unkind words that were spoken to you?

Ear-related verbs: eavesdropped, overheard, heard the words of, heard the music of, heard _____'s voice, listened to, listened for, ignored.

Mouth

- What are your favorite foods?

- Have you ever sung to an audience or given a speech?

- Do you like to chew gum?

- Do you have a "sweet tooth"? Do you crave any sweets in particular?

- What makes your mouth "water"?

- Have you ever "held your tongue"? Have you ever wanted so badly to yell at someone or tell them something but instead you held it in?

- Do you have any "acquired tastes"? Are there unique or exotic foods you enjoy that many people don't?

- Have you ever lip-synched before, or been in a lip-synching contest?

- Have you ever been good at "tongue twisters"?

- Can you twist or curl your tongue?

- Who are people you love that you have kissed?

Mouth-related verbs: tasted, ate, salivated, chewed, whistled, breathed, bit, licked, swallowed, kissed, whispered, shouted, sang, screamed, muttered, swore.

Voice

- Have you ever recited, sung, or performed something in public?
- Have you ever had a secret language?
- Have you ever shared a secret?
- What songs can you sing best?
- Tell about a time you screamed in delight.
- Have you ever sung to a child, a pet, or a loved one?
- What swear words have you said and what made you use them?
- What makes you laugh?
- How would you describe your voice?

Voice-related verbs: said, shouted, screamed, sang, hummed, whispered, swore, whimpered, muttered, whined, complained, complimented.

Spirit

- What have you hoped and wished for?
- Have you ever witnessed a miracle?
- Have you ever experienced something paranormal?
- Have you ever experienced clairvoyance, precognition, or another extrasensory experience?
- Have you ever been present during a birth or a death of someone? What about for a pet or animal?
- What, if anything, have you had repetitive dreams about?
- What (nighttime) dreams have you had that have stuck with you?
- What music, art, or written words makes you feel more alive and connected?
- Do you have any animal totems, angels, guides, or other spiritual companions?
- Have you ever been to a psychic, had a past life regression, or had your tarot cards read?
- Have you ever been to church?
- Do you have any spiritual or religious role models?
- Do you believe in life after death?

- Have you ever meditated?

- Have you ever healed something within yourself or someone else?

- Have you ever seen yourself as having more than one identity?

- Have you ever gone through a major change in your life or learned a key lesson?

- What feeds your soul? What do you need in your life to feel like your authentic self?

Spirit-related verbs: grieved, mourned, felt the presence of _____, prayed, meditated, imagined, visualized, survived, exiled, departed from, entered, ascended, descended, sensed, tuned in to, released, healed, healed from, travelled to, journeyed to, dreamed, received a message from, exulted, pondered, envisioned, protested, created, transformed, metamorphosed, transitioned, enchanted, regenerated, transmuted, opened, changed, grew.

Reflect on your list. Do you think about yourself or your body any differently for enduring anything or everything on your list? Do you have any renewed respect for things you've accomplished, for things you've survived, or for unique experiences that you alone have had?

When you are done reflecting on your list, thank your body for all the gifts and positive experiences it has provided to you.

▶ SELFIES

Selfies are photos that people take of themselves. They can be done in many formats and styles, shared with others, or kept private. For some, selfies are an enjoyable activity. For others, selfies can be a challenge, especially for those who do not like how they look, or have a distorted sense of how they look. They can also be a challenge for those who do not fit the "norm" of what their culture expects them to look like. Whether you are comfortable with selfies or not, this activity uses selfies as a means for exploring your unique beauty.

- First, take a moment to reflect on your own unique physical attributes and personal style. If possible, ignore any thoughts that come into your head about what your culture, your peer group, your family, societal norms, fashion trends, etc. say you "should" look like. Pretend these societal expectations do not exist. Pretend that every single physical attribute is beautiful and culturally accepted, and that however you choose to dress and accessorize is also accepted. How would you choose to take a selfie then? Would it be any different than the way you take them now? Try taking pictures of yourself as if there were no risks in being judged for them. These selfies are solely for you and for no one else, unless you choose to share them.

- Focus on a small and precise detail on your face or body that you like or find interesting and take a photo of it—it can be one freckle, or a cluster of freckles, the outer corner of your eye, your pupil, the palm of your hand, a mole, a scar, the arch of your foot, a flexed muscle, a birthmark, your hair, a pierced ear, an eyebrow, the bridge of your nose, etc. Take as many photos as you like. As you look over your photos, give yourself positive feedback (you can do this in your head, you do not need to say anything out loud). For example, tell yourself that these individual aspects of your face and body are beautiful, lovely, unique, compelling, curious, or striking.

- If negative thoughts and self criticism pop into your mind, remind yourself that beauty is viewed differently all across the world; that even if you find any of these parts unattractive there are many people who find them beautiful; that when you are older looking back at these photos you will most likely say to yourself, "Wow, I wish I knew then what I know now—I can now see the beauty in myself back then;" or remind yourself that many people struggle with how they look, and you are not alone in this. Also, if you have ever looked up to someone, such as a mentor, a teacher, or someone famous (athlete, author, world leader, religious or spiritual leader, etc.), think about whether it mattered to you how they looked. Did you even notice? Do you think they ever looked in the mirror and struggled with a perceived physical "imperfection"? Remind yourself that you are human—just like the very people you look up to, regardless of how they look. You are beautiful simply because you are you.

▶ BEYOND REPORT CARDS

Some students feel misunderstood, invisible, or under-appreciated at school. They may feel judged by their report cards, grades, and testing scores more than their personal strengths or the day-to-day challenges they overcome. An "ideal student" is often regarded as the one who comes to school on time, attends classes with focus and attention, receives good grades, and is obedient in following the rules. But if you are a student who has challenges at home (e.g. a family member has an addiction, there's domestic violence, the family is living in poverty, etc.) or challenges within yourself (e.g. a learning disability, anxiety, sensory overload, etc.), getting to school and sitting through the school day may be an insurmountable achievement. To add an expectation on top of that you should thrive and get good grades can be rather overwhelming and even unrealistic. Oftentimes these are students who get labeled, unfairly judged, or even ignored (and sometimes no one is aware of what the student is going through).

I wanted to include this section to remind you that, if you are a student who struggles with school or grades on any level, you are not your report card. You are a valued human being, doing your best with what you have.

Look over the "Personal Strengths List" handout and highlight the ones that describe you. Also highlight the strengths that others would say you have.

If you ever find yourself feeling negative about yourself or upset with how others perceive you, look over your list and remind yourself that you have many admirable strengths.

Personal Strengths List

Active	Creative	Good listener
Adventurous	Curious	Grateful
Affectionate	Daring	Hardworking
Agile	Decisive	Healthy
Ambitious	Dependable	Helpful
Appreciative	Determined	Honest
Athletic	Devoted	Hopeful
Brave	Eager	Humble
Brilliant	Easy-going	Humorous
Calm	Efficient	Imaginative
Candid	Empathic	Independent
Capable	Energetic	Innovative
Carefree	Enthusiastic	Inquisitive
Caring	Ethical	Intelligent
Cautious	Fair	Inventive
Charming	Faithful	Joyful
Civil	Fearless	Kind
Clever	Focused	Logical
Compassionate	Forgiving	Lovable
Concerned	Friendly	Loving
Confident	Funny	Loyal
Conscientious	Generous	Lucky
Considerate	Gentle	Mature
Cooperative	Good friend	Modest

*

Non-judgmental	Quick	Supportive
Obedient	Quiet	Sweet
Observant	Rational	Talented
Open-minded	Realistic	Tenacious
Optimistic	Reliable	Thoughtful
Organized	Respectful	Tolerant
Passionate	Responsible	Tough
Patient	Safe	Trusting
Peaceful	Self-respecting	Trustworthy
Pensive	Sensitive	Understanding
Perceptive	Silly	Unpretentious
Persistent	Sincere	Versatile
Persuasive	Skillful	Warm-hearted
Pleasant	Smart	Wise
Polite	Sociable	Witty
Protective	Strong	
Proud	Studious	

▶ SHARING THE POWER OF ACCEPTANCE

Regardless of how a person was born, how they look, any challenges they have, the amount of money they own, etc., they have positive qualities. Acceptance is the ability to see those qualities in others.

You can practice the power of acceptance by complimenting others about the positive things you see in them. When you compliment and honor other people's strengths, you help them feel better about themselves. When you help others feel good about themselves, it gives them—and you—a self esteem boost.

You can use the "Personal Strengths List" handout to remind you of the strengths to recognize in others. Here are some examples:

"That was…of you" [kind, generous, smart, clever]

"I appreciate your…" [sense of humor, kindness, generosity, attention to this matter, open mind, uniqueness]

"I admire your…" [ability to solve problems, talents, tenacity, focus, creativity, honesty, dedication, loyalty]

"You're so…—thank you!" [sweet, generous, patient, understanding]

Practice recognizing other people's strengths—share the power of acceptance and see how good it makes you feel.

▶ THIS IS MY DECLARATION

A declaration is a statement about who you are and what you represent. It includes—but isn't limited to—the things you believe, value, embrace, strive for, stand up for, resist and/ or fight against. A declaration is also a creative way to explore what your core values are.

You can use the "This is My Declaration" worksheet to write your own. You can also add any other ideas, values, beliefs, etc. to your declaration that are not already covered here.

Once your declaration is complete, hang it up to remind yourself of all that you strive for and embrace. If you want to take this activity a step further, turn your declaration into a piece of artwork or poster.

*

This is My Declaration
· ·

Fill in the sections below to create your personal declaration.

My name is _____ and this is my declaration:

I believe…

I value…

I embrace…

I strive for…

I stand up for…

I resist…

And I fight for…

Create healthy relationships

Take a moment to reflect on what a "healthy relationship" means to you. You can do this on your own or you can have a discussion about it with a close friend or family member. Consider the following:

- What words come to mind when you hear the phrase "healthy relationship"?

- If you've had an unhealthy relationship with someone, what would you say was unhealthy about it?

- If you've had a healthy relationship with someone, what stands out as healthy about it?

- Do you think a relationship can have unhealthy patterns in it and, overall, still be a healthy relationship?

- Have you ever had a relationship with someone where a friend or loved one expressed concern that the other person was not treating you well? If so, did you understand why that person was concerned?

- Has anyone ever told you that you were not treating them well? If so, did you understand why that person thought so?

The following activities will help you expand on the definition of a healthy relationship and suggest ways for developing healthy relationships with others.

▶ GREEN, YELLOW, RED BEHAVIORS

Think about traffic lights for a moment. A green light means "go," yellow means "slow down—caution," and red means "stop." If you applied the same color code to behaviors in a relationship, you might say that "green behaviors" are those that are safe and respectful and that feel good to continue, "yellow behaviors" are those that cause you to slow down or pause, and "red behaviors" are those that are unsafe, disrespectful, or unkind and that you want to stop.

To explore these behaviors further, complete the worksheet "Green, Yellow, Red Behaviors" and then think about, or discuss, the following:

LOOK OVER THE BEHAVIORS UNDERLINED IN RED

- If you noticed any of these behaviors in someone you were just getting to know, would you distance yourself from that person? Why, or why not?

- How do you respond when a friend, or someone you're in a relationship with, says something mean to you? Do you wish you could respond in another way? If so, how?

- Think of a time when someone acted unkind or unsafe and you distanced yourself from that person. How do you feel about that choice now? For example, do you feel you made the right choice?

- Think of a time someone acted unkind or unsafe and you stayed with that person. How do you feel about that choice now? For example, do you feel you made the right choice?

- What are your thoughts and feelings about family members who act unkind or unsafe?

- Think about your own behaviors—do you tend to show more or fewer red behaviors to others?

- Which of your own red behaviors do you want to get rid of?

LOOK OVER THE BEHAVIORS UNDERLINED IN GREEN

- Who in your life, if anyone, shows mostly green behaviors to you?

- Who in your life do you feel safe with?

- Who do you wish would show you more behaviors underlined in green?

- Think about your own behaviors—do you tend to show more or fewer green behaviors to others?

LOOK OVER THE BEHAVIORS UNDERLINED IN YELLOW

- Who in your life, if anyone, shows mostly yellow behaviors to you? How would you describe this person?

- What is it like (or what would it be like) to be around someone who shows mostly yellow behaviors?

- Do you think other people would describe any of your behaviors as yellow?

Use this reflection to think about how you want others to treat you, and how you want to treat others. When you find yourself struggling with a relationship for one reason or another, it may help to come back to the completed worksheet and look at these behaviors again. You may find that some of the behaviors you underlined in yellow and red are contributing to a challenging relationship and may provide clarity about whether the relationship is heading in a healthy (or unhealthy) direction.

Green, Yellow, Red Behaviors

Look over the list of behaviors.

Highlight or underline behaviors that are respectful and healthy with a *green* marker.

Highlight or underline behaviors that are disrespectful and unhealthy with a *red* marker.

Highlight or underline the remaining behaviors in *yellow*.

A person I know…

Shows kindness.

Listens to me.

Looks at their phone a lot when we're spending time together.

Asks me what I need to feel safe.

Earns my trust (rather than demanding it).

Yells at me.

Gives me gifts on special occasions.

Gives me gifts when they make a mistake or hurt me.

Encourages me to follow my dreams/meet my goals.

Calls me names I don't want to be called/names I don't like.

Calls me nicknames I like.

Can disagree with me without resorting to threats or being mean.

Is honest with me.

Ignores me.

Checks on me several times a day.

Sends me nice messages.

Pushes me (physically).

Hits me.

Is playful with me.

Gets angry and/or jealous when I hang out with other people.

Encourages me to do well in school.

Tells me I'm not good enough.

Trusts me.

Tries to "fix" me.

Is happy for me when something goes right for me.

Touches me or kisses me, and I enjoy it.

Touches me or kisses me, and I don't enjoy it.

Asks me to send them pictures of my body.

Asks to borrow money and doesn't repay me.

Asks to borrow money.

Threatens to hurt themself if I won't spend time with them anymore.

Celebrates or recognizes my birthday.

► RELATIONSHIP JOB DESCRIPTIONS

When you apply for a job you usually see a job title and job description that goes with it. The job description is where the expectations of the job are listed in detail. Relationships are similar to jobs in that they also have titles and expectations that go with the type of relationship.

For this activity you write out "job descriptions" for different relationships (see the "Relationship Job Descriptions" worksheet). Relationships include all the connections you have with others in various roles (e.g. as a sibling, a friend, a coworker, a neighbor, etc.).

Look at the following list of relationship titles and write a brief job description for what you expect or want from each of these relationships. Consider expectations such as: this person needs to be trustworthy; this person needs to respect boundaries and privacy; if I'm sick this person will help take care of me; I need to be able to call this person in an emergency.

RELATIONSHIP TITLES

Best friend

Friend

Someone I'm dating/in a relationship with

A parent

A sibling

A coworker or classmate I spend a lot of time with

A friend online I've never met personally

A neighbor

There are several reasons for exploring this topic. (1) It helps you to recognize what it is you expect from others. (2) By defining your expectations you develop a sense of your own relational boundaries and what you need from others. (3) Once you know what you expect from others, you can communicate it to others. Communication about your expectations in a relationship can save a lot of miscommunication, confusion, and heartache later on. And (4), by defining your own boundaries and expectations, you may also become more sensitive to others' boundaries and expectations.

*

Relationship Job Descriptions

Circle one of the following relationship roles:

Mother

Father

Sister

Brother

Stepmother

Stepfather

Stepsister

Stepbrother

Friend

Best friend

Foster parent

Girlfriend/boyfriend

Other: _____

Write a "job description" for the role you circled. What do you expect from a person in this role?

_____

_____

_____

_____

_____

_____

Do you think your job description is a fair and reasonable one for someone in this role?

▶ THE FRIENDSHIP WHEEL

"The Friendship Wheel" helps you evaluate the spectrum and depth of your friendships. It's an informative activity because it helps you see how one friendship differs from another. It also helps you put in perspective which friends, if any, you can trust with a secret or which ones you feel comfortable crying in front of, for example.

The worksheet displays a circle divided into 16 sections. Each section has a statement and color label—if the statement matches your friend and/or relationship, color it in with the designated color. When you've finished the 16 sections, and colored in the ones that match your friend, your wheel is done. You can complete as many Friendship Wheels as you like, but make sure to label the wheel with your friend's name and do one wheel per friend.

Whether you complete one wheel or several, you can learn a lot about your friendships. Here are some insights other tweens and teens have shared after finishing their wheels:

"I don't have any friends I would trust with a secret."

"I now wonder how my friends would color a wheel about me."

"All of my friends make me laugh—that must be something I really need or look for in a friend."

" I can see why my mom doesn't like this one friend—I barely colored any of that wheel."

"I can see why my parents like this friend [most of the wheel is colored in] and keep saying I should spend more time with him."

Note: You can color half of a section if the quality noted in that section pertains to your friend some of the time. For example, if you have a friend who makes you laugh once in while, but not often, you can fill that section in half-way with the designated color.

The Friendship Wheel

FRIEND'S NAME: _____

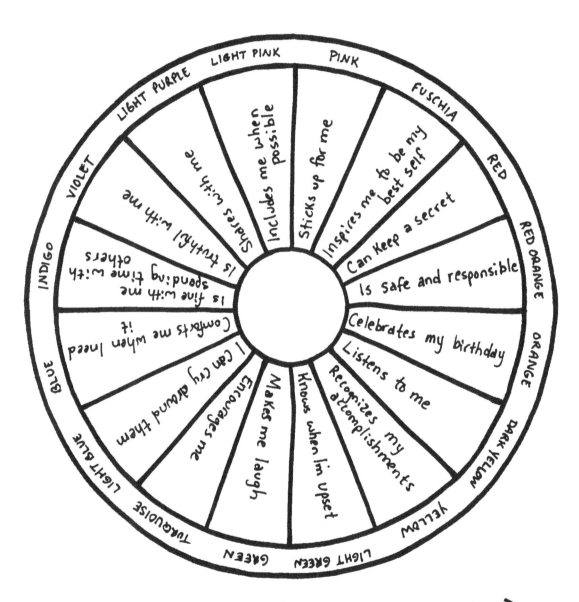

Color in the areas (with assigned colors)
if they describe your friend.

▶ BALANCED DISCOURSE

Discourse is having a discussion about a topic. Some topics are relatively easy to discuss with friends and family, while other topics might feel tense or conflictual. In many areas of the world we've become less skilled at having "balanced discourse." Balanced discourse means hearing and discussing more than one point of view without the need for polarizing the issue or needing to take sides with one person or another. There are some cases where it makes sense to take one side, but oftentimes there are two or more sides to a situation. If you're only listening to one side of the situation, then you're not getting the full story.

When people are taking part in balanced discourse you might hear comments within the conversation such as:

"I hear what you're saying. I don't agree with what you said about…but I do see where you are coming from."

"We see different sides of this issue."

"I can disagree with you on this and still respect you."

"This is a tough conversation to have because we both see things so differently. But I'm glad we're talking about it so we can understand each other's point of view better."

The reason that balanced discourse is critical to wellbeing is because it helps us understand ourselves, our friends and loved ones, and the world much better. We need to be able to talk about our experiences, thoughts, and feelings about what is going in our own lives and the lives of others. Balanced discourse creates more understanding among people and leads to a platform for solving conflicts in a more peaceful manner.

Here are some reminders about balanced discourse that I often say to youth:

People can disagree with you and still like who you are.

You can disagree with someone else's thought and opinions and still treat them with respect.

It's normal for people to disagree with one another, to have thoughts, feelings, and opinions different than your own.

Every person has their own side of the story. Sometimes two people experience the same event differently.

In situations where the event or situation involved abuse or violence, bring in trusted adults and/or professionals.

Use the "Balanced Discourse" worksheet to help you organize your thoughts about a discussion with friends or loved ones. If more than three people are involved in the discussion, copy extra worksheets as needed to include each person. Don't forget to include yourself.

Balanced Discourse

TOPIC: _____ _____ _____	Name of person in the discussion: _____ _____	Name of person in the discussion: _____ _____	Name of person in the discussion: _____ _____
Their side of the story or topic:			
They said they feel:			
We agree on this:			
We disagree on this:			

▶ HOW TO DEAL WITH BULLYING

Bullying and abuse is when a person harms another person.

Types of behaviors associated with bullying and relational abuse include: control and coercion, belittling, name calling, intimidating, manipulating, denying something that was said or done, and more. It can look like any of the following:

- A person does something on purpose to cause you harm in the form of embarrassment/humiliation, physical pain, or making you feel shame, fear, terror, belittled, or bad about yourself, etc.

- The person has no recognition or remorse for the harm they caused.

- The person blames you or someone else for the harm they caused.

- The person tells you to "get over it," "it wasn't a big deal," or they tell you you're overreacting.

- They deny what happened.

- They threaten you not to tell anyone else they harmed you.

- They blackmail or manipulate you into keeping quiet about it.

However, a person who is truly sorry for their action, and/or mature enough to understand the harm they caused, will:

- acknowledge and own their behavior

- recognize the impact their behavior had on the other person

- apologize for their actions

- do their best to amend and heal what they can

- respect the boundaries of the person they hurt by giving them the time and space to earn the trust back (if it can happen).

So what are you supposed to do if someone you know is bullying you or being abusive? Here are some suggestions:

- Remind yourself you do not deserve to be treated this way.

- Tell the other person that what they are doing makes you uncomfortable and/or tell them to stop the behavior (be specific, if you can). For example, "Calling me [that word] is hurtful—stop calling me that;" "I want you to delete that video you took of me—it embarrasses me and I don't want others to see it;" "I don't want to be touched that way—please stop;" "I don't like it when you treat me like that. It's hurtful. Please stop."

- If the person does not listen to you and/or continues to act in this manner, stop spending time with them (if feasible).

- You may need to block them from all social media.

- Document what is happening. If any of the abuse and bullying is happening online, screen shot everything right away before the person can delete it.

- Tell a trusted adult what is happening.

- Inform authorities as needed to let them know what is going on. Authorities can include a school resource office, school administrator or superintendent, the local police, a community leader, etc.

- Document every contact you have with authority about the matter—write down the dates and time when you met with them and who you spoke to. Keep any paperwork they give you.

- Be kind and respectful to others—it will be hard for people to take you seriously if you yourself are doing anything considered bullying or abusive.

- If, at any time, you think your personal safety is at risk, contact your local emergency services and/or the police. You may need to file a restraining order or similar documentation depending on what country or municipality you live in.

If you're not sure whether you're in a relationship where abuse and/or bullying is happening, seek support and guidance from a trusted adult.

▶ HOW TO SAY "NO" AND SET BOUNDARIES

"Boundaries" are the guidelines you establish for yourself regarding what you will and will not tolerate and how you expect others to treat you. Setting boundaries means letting others know what those guidelines are. For instance, it can include telling someone, "No, I won't do that;" "I will not lie for you or anyone else;" "I want you to be honest with me;" "I don't like it when you do that/say that;" "I need to know that if I come to you and ask for help that you will listen to me and believe me."

Adults often tell me how difficult it is for them to say "no" to others and set appropriate boundaries, so it's no surprise to me that teens and tweens have similar challenges. Here are comments I hear from youth about setting boundaries:

"I have no time to myself lately and I'm feeling really stressed out. I just want to stay home Friday night but my friend will be really mad if I don't go to the dance with her."

"He asked me out and I said yes. But I wanted to say no."

"Ever since my parents split up they talk badly about each other and argue in front of me. It makes me mad and uncomfortable. I feel like I'm being pulled in two different directions."

"My friend is making bad choices and I don't want to be around that behavior. I don't know how to talk to her about it."

There are many reasons why saying "no" and setting boundaries can feel challenging—e.g. if you're worried about hurting someone's feelings; if you don't live in a community or culture where advocating for your needs is accepted; if you seek to please others to the extent that you put others' needs before your own (even if your need is greater); if you're afraid of conflict or difficult conversations; if you don't know what you need; or if you're not used to stating your needs. There are more reasons, but hopefully these provide some insight into what makes saying "no" and setting boundaries so challenging.

If you haven't done so already, the worksheet "Relationship Job Descriptions" is a nice place to start in terms of defining what you expect from the various relationships and people in your life. In addition, the worksheet "This is My Declaration" helps you outline what you yourself believe in and stand for.

Other strategies to help you say "no" and set boundaries with others include:

- Make a list of the times you said "yes" or "no" to something (or someone) when you really wanted to say the opposite. Write down how you felt in each situation where you didn't listen to your own boundaries and needs.

- When someone asks you to do something, say "I need to think about that" rather than giving a quick "yes" or "no." By giving yourself time to think about it, you can be better prepared to stand your ground and provide a firm response.

- Practice saying "no." You can practice by yourself just by saying it out loud. Repeat the word "no" or you can sing it, shout it, scream it, say it in funny voices, etc. The point is just to get familiar saying it.

- Practice setting boundaries. Ask a friend or loved one to ask you ridiculous things to do to which you reply by stating boundaries, even if they're fictional ones (e.g. Friend: "Would you like to go to the 'all-you-can-eat' sea cucumber buffet?" You: "No thank you. That's not something I'd enjoy.")

Build community

Although some people use the term "community" to describe the actual place where they live, I use the word "community" to describe a group of people that share similar passions, interests, ideas, traditions, beliefs, and/or similar goals. The people in this type of community may or may not live in the same area or ever meet in the same place at all.

Building community for yourself is important for a few reasons: community provides an ongoing opportunity to build positive relationships with others; it allows for networking that may help you get a new job, scholarship, or other opportunity; you can learn from others who are interested in the same topics and pursuits as yourself; it's a great way to meet people of different backgrounds, ages, economic status, influence, and so on; you can get support and encouragement from community members; and you have a sense of belonging.

Some people find community among peers, their family, their church, an athletic team, or their school. Others, however, need to work harder to find a community or group of people they feel comfortable with. If you ever feel alone or disconnected from others, it doesn't mean you don't belong—it means you haven't found your community yet. There are people all over the world who have similar (or the same) interests and ideas as you, and sometimes it takes a bit of work to find them. Here are ideas for how to define and create a community for yourself.

▶ FINDING AND BUILDING YOUR PERSONAL COMMUNITY

- Start with yourself. If you haven't done so yet, do the "This is My Declaration" worksheet. This guides you to explore your beliefs, passions, ideas, and strengths that define who you are. If you want to find like-minded people, it helps to know yourself first.

- Create a list of your current community. Write down the names of people you feel any connection with. You can include friends, family, school staff, neighbors, teammates, church members, club members, family friends, etc.

- List any friends, acquaintances, or peers you have shared a connection or commonality with. Some people include animals in their community. If you want to add animals you have a special connection with, then do so.

- Look over your list so far. Do you have any interests, beliefs, or goals not represented in your community yet? If so, you can always work on expanding your community:

  — Join an extracurricular club at school—if your school doesn't offer any clubs that you're interested in, advocate for a new one. Some schools offer clubs for social activism, animal rights, civil rights, robotics, LGBTQ, writing groups, fashion, drama, math competitions, debate teams, and more.

— Join an athletic team.

— Volunteer in your community.

— Get a new job—this is a great way to meet new people.

— Take a class outside of your school (e.g. take a babysitting course, a dance class, a music lesson).

— Go to your local library—see what they offer for people your age. Many libraries now have innovative opportunities for tweens and teens such as gaming groups and coding classes.

— Start a book club.

— Join a support group—if you have a particular challenge in your life, these groups can provide ongoing support from others going through the same thing as you. If there is not a support group to meet your need, ask a trusted adult about how to get one started. Sometimes hospitals, community agencies, counselors, places of worship/churches, libraries and school support staff can be places to request a certain group.

WORKING WITH COMMUNITY

Niki Willows

We live by the sea in England and we have a great surfing beach that the whole village uses. Some people walk their dogs there, the kids bodyboard or surf, and we all picnic and play in the sand. But our beach is on the north coast of Cornwall and gets hit by the Atlantic waves (which is why it's good for surfing!). This also brings in lots of marine litter from the sea. It gets dumped on our beach and eaten by sea birds, and when it's in the sea, it gets eaten by fish, seals, and marine mammals. Seals can also get really tangled up in old fishing net and lines which we call ghost gear. Every now and then we organize a community beach clean. We meet on the beach armed with buckets, gloves, and bin bags. We start one end of the strandline and work our way across the beach, picking up anything that shouldn't be there. We like to see who can find the strangest thing—we've found a false fingernail with stars on it, Kinder Egg toys, LEGO®, a flare from a lifeboat, and little rubber fish used for lures in fishing. We pile all the rubbish up and stack it in the bin bags; our local council are great at taking it away for us. Everyone says "Ooooh, I thought it was a clean beach" or "I had no idea how much rubbish there was" because our beach looks tidy, but in the sand are tiny bits of broken-down plastic and little lentil-sized pellets. The latter are called mermaid's tears or nurdles and are spilt from shipping containers tipping off ships in rough weather. We feel good as a community when we've worked together. I organize the beach cleans for a charity called Surfers Against Sewage, but anyone can get some friends and family together and clean their beach or street. You just need to turn up and do it.

LIBRARIES AND THE COMMUNITY REVOLUTION

Megan Emery[2]

Do you know what a library does? If your first thought had to do with books, you're wrong. If your first thought was "shhhhh," you really need to dust off your library card and get back in there!

The modern library has been steadily staging a community revolution, updating our offerings to reflect our communities' needs and interests. Sure, we've still got the stuff you're familiar with in a library—books, movies, computers, music, and classes—but we've hit the refresh button on all that stuff. Classes now tackle how to start coding, how to actually create those projects you've got saved in Pinterest, or how to start a successful business even if you aren't legally an adult yet. In some libraries, like mine, patrons are given control of our purchasing so you can shop for the books, movies, and music you want, add it to our collection, and then be the first person who gets to borrow it. Our spaces now reflect the need for more tactile learning incorporating maker spaces brimming with laser cutters, sewing machines, 3D printers, vinyl cutters, woodworking or metalworking tools, recording studios, repair spaces, bicycle tuning stations, teaching kitchens, and a seemingly unlimited amount of art and craft supplies. Gone is the "shhhh" and taking its place is the joyous noise that comes from exploration.

Personally, when people ask me what a librarian does in the age of Google, Netflix, and smartphones, I tell them "Librarians are conduits to the universe." A universe of interests, opportunities to explore, new hobbies, mentors, brilliant ideas that exists inside of you is waiting to be discovered. That universe is bigger than books, and so are we.

As you can imagine, when you're offering up "The Universe" on a silver platter, some pretty interesting people come knocking. In my time working in libraries I've worked with fashion designers, inventors, painters, computer programmers, soap makers, medieval scholars, police officers, puppeteers, graffiti artists, musicians, teachers, therapists, zookeepers, marketing specialists, robot builders, cosplayers, environmentalists, farmers, jewelers, weavers, tea makers, architects, mail carriers, nutritionists, dancers, makeup artists, senators, and more. These folk have given talks and workshops, led and assisted with classes, showcased their creative processes, given lessons to staff, and sometimes just hang out at the library because it's so massively cool now.

Finding your tribe is tricky at any age, but libraries are facilitating opportunities for you to follow the breadcrumbs of your passions straight to your own tribe. I've seen so many friendships, relationships, and positive opportunities for our communities come about because people met up at the library. I've seen people get jobs, stage protests to improve their lives, and learn the skills they need to build their own home. I've seen people from diverse backgrounds discover common ground, create handmade gifts for their loved ones

---

2 Author of *Cooking Up Library Programs Teens and Tweens Will Love: Recipes for Success*; librarian at Chattanooga Public Library System.

instead of buying them, and host birthday parties in our space because it's their favorite place in our entire city.

The revolution of your universe is here and the library is waiting to be your guide. Let's hang out and do something cool together!

3
Coping Skills

. . . .

Coping skills are interventions you can use to help you manage difficult feelings, moments, or events. Some coping skills help you calm your body and mind; other coping skills help you focus or stay in the moment.

Times when coping skills can be helpful:

- If you feel emotionally upset or disregulated.

- If you feel overwhelmed.

- If your brain is too busy or overloaded.

- If you're transitioning from one activity to another (e.g. before heading out the door to school or work).

- If you're adjusting to something new (e.g. a new home, new teacher, someone new living in your home).

- If you're angry and you need/want to calm down.

- If you're preparing for an event that you feel nervous about (e.g. taking a test or trying out for a team).

- If you're feeling anxious.

- If you've recently been through an emotional or traumatic experience.

- If you experience depersonalization:

People who are suffering from depersonalization feel separated from their own physicality, meaning that their own feelings, emotions, bodily sensations and movements feel detached from themselves. (Pedersen 2018a)

- If you experience derealization:

A person's perception of reality is altered in such a way that everything feels unfamiliar or unreal. Derealization is typically not a stand-alone disorder, but a side effect of severe anxiety, panic or certain types of drug use or withdrawal. It may also occur with some neurological disorders, such as epilepsy, head injury or migraine. (Pedersen 2018b)

- If you experience disassociation:

Dissociation is a mental process that causes a lack of connection in a person's thoughts, memory and sense of identity. Dissociation seems to fall on a continuum of severity. Mild dissociation would be like daydreaming, getting 'lost' in a book, or when you are driving down a familiar stretch of road and realize that you do not remember the last several miles. (Mental Health America n.d.)

This chapter reviews these various coping skills:

- Breathe
- Try a hand mudra
- Practice grounding
- Do a body scan
- Use distraction
- Get outside in nature
- Burn off adrenaline
- Release tension
- Take a break
- Use aromatherapy
- Have a calming bath
- Use fidgets
- Listen to music
- Use visualization
- Create art

- Release what doesn't help you

- Reframe your thoughts

- Focus on what you have control of

- Ask for help

- Scales

- Use reminders for self care and coping

Use the worksheet titled "Coping and Calming Skills Track Sheet" to document the coping and calming skills you try and how well they work. This will make it easier for you to know which skills help and which ones don't. Once you've tried several skills and have found some that help, make sure to include those skills in any coping plans, self-care kits, and so on covered in the "Use reminders for self care and coping skills" section of the book.

Coping and Calming Skills Track Sheet

Coping and calming skills	Mark an "x" if you've tried it	Mark an "x" if it helped you feel calmer or better (even if just a little bit)

Breathe

A common side effect of stress and tension is holding your breath or breathing shallow. You can counteract this side effect with basic breathing techniques. Give the following techniques a try and see if any of them improve your breathing and/or help you feel calmer.

> **Note:** Dizziness and lightheadedness can happen if you start to breathe too much—yes, there's such a thing—it's called hyperventilation. Hyperventilation is a cue to your body that the technique is not being done correctly or is not a good match for your body. If at any time you start to feel dizzy or lightheaded using any breathing technique, stop and take a break. If you find breathing exercises consistently troublesome, let your healthcare provider know so they can help address why.

▶ ALTERNATE NOSTRIL BREATHING

Alternate nostril breathing is when you breathe in through one nostril and out through the other. It's a bit tricky to get the rhythm of it at first, but once you practice a few times, you'll get the hang of it.

DIRECTIONS

- Gently place your right thumb on the right side of your nose, and your right pointer finger on the left side of your nose.

- Press your thumb against the right side of your nose while you breathe in through your left nostril.

- Exhale out of your right nostril while pressing on your left nostril.

- Keep this position and inhale through your right nostril.

- Press your thumb against the right side of your nose while you exhale through your left nostril.

- Keep this position and inhale through your left nostril.

- Exhale out of your right nostril while pressing on your left nostril.

- Keep this position and inhale through your right nostril.

- Press your thumb against the right side of your nose while you exhale through your left nostril.

- Keep this position and inhale through your left nostril.

- Repeat as needed.

▶ PATTERNED BREATHING

Patterned breathing is when you breathe in and out to the count of a specific number. For example, "Breathe in to the count of three…now breathe out to the count of three." Some people are able to comfortably breathe in and out to the count of four, but for others, that number might be two or five. What's important is finding the right number for you.

- Practice breathing in and out at a comfortable pace. Count (in your head) as you inhale and exhale. Notice the most common number that you count to as you inhale and then exhale.

- Next, continue to breathe in and out to that same number for a repetition of three times.

- How did that feel? If you felt lightheaded while trying this, lower the number you counted to.

- After a few minutes try this again. How did it feel this time? The goal is to find a comfortable but focused pace for breathing in and out.

- When you do find the number that feels best, remember this pattern for times when you need to take a deep breath, relax, and refocus.

▶ BLOWING BUBBLES

Blowing bubbles (of the liquid kind) helps you to practice controlled breathing. Controlled breathing is a nice skill to learn, especially if you're the type of person who holds their breath or hyperventilates when feeling stress. When you practice controlling your breath you become more familiar with the cues your body gives you regarding your own breath. Since blowing bubbles requires you to control your breath in order to get different sizes and number of bubbles, it's a simple but fun way to practice. To get the best practice, try blowing the largest bubbles that you can, and then try blowing the smallest bubbles that you can.

THE THREE-PART BREATH

Karla Helbert, LPC, E-RYT, C-IAYT[1]

The three-part breath, *deergha swasam*

The three-part breath is a specific breathing technique used in yoga practices. *Deergha swasam* means "complete breath." It can be very useful in times of stress or whenever you need to relax. This type of breathing stimulates the parasympathetic nervous system, the relaxation response, and allows your body and mind to more easily release stress and tension. Practicing the three-part breath before bed can be very helpful with sleep problems.

In typical breathing, we use only about one third of our lungs' capacity. With *deergha swasam*, we can increase the amount of oxygen we are taking in by up to 70 percent. This can be soothing to the mind and can induce almost immediate calm. If you feel dizzy or lightheaded while practicing the three-part breath, or any other breathing exercise, stop the practice immediately and allow your breathing to go back to normal. Find your comfortable sitting position, allowing your hands to be relaxed. The three-part breath may also be done lying down. To begin, inhale. Then, with your mouth closed, exhale slowly through your nose as you did with the simple deep breathing exercises, using your abdominal muscles to pull your diaphragm inward. Squeeze all the stale, excess air completely out of your lungs.

As you prepare for your next inhalation, imagine your upper body as a large pitcher. As you inhale, you are filling the pitcher from bottom to top. As you inhale, fill the diaphragm and lower belly, allowing them to expand and completely fill with air. Next, continue to allow the pitcher to fill as you notice the lower, and then the upper, parts of the ribcage expanding outward and up. Finally, fill the upper lungs, noticing the chest expanding, the collar bones and shoulders rising, as the pitcher is filled completely to the top. Pause for two counts.

Exhale in the opposite way, allowing the pitcher to empty from top to bottom. As you slowly exhale, allow the shoulders and collar bones to slowly drop, the chest to deflate and the ribs to move inward. Pull your diaphragm in, using it to completely empty the air from the bottom of the lungs. Repeat the process, re-filling the pitcher slowly from bottom to top. Continue with complete and full exhalations and inhalations, emptying and filling your pitcher.

The three parts are bottom, middle, top—expanding as you slowly and completely fill your body with fresh, cell-nourishing, life-giving oxygen, and then contracting slowly as you the lungs of carbon dioxide, toxins, and tension held in the body and mind. Ideally, the exhalations should be about twice as long as the inhalations. Initially, if you count to five as you inhale and exhale, gradually try to make your exhalations to a count of six, then seven, then eight, and so on, until you feel more comfortable lengthening your exhalations.

---

1   Author of *Yoga for Grief and Loss: Poses, Meditation, Devotion, Self-Reflection, Selfless Acts, Ritual* and *Finding Your Own Way to Grieve: A Creative Activity Workbook for Kids and Teens on the Autism Spectrum.*

Try a hand mudra

Hand mudras are yoga positions specifically for your hands and fingers. There are many different mudras including ones that improve focus, heighten intuition, and induce relaxation. There are also hand mudras for physical ailments. What I like most about hand mudras is they can often be done while sitting in class or in other public spaces.

Mudras can be done for a set amount of time, for example 45 minutes at a time or in three sittings of 15 minutes. Other mudras might be held until the symptoms subside. The following hand mudra is called the *Dhyana mudra*. It's a mudra for concentration and tranquility:

> The Dhyana mudra is shared across several eastern meditation disciplines. The Buddha is often pictured doing this gesture. The significance of this mudra is to bring you into deeper, more profound concentration. This gesture can also help bring you tranquility and inner peace.
>
> Method: To do the Dhyana mudra, simply sit with your hands facing upward, right hand resting on top of your left palm. The right hand, representing enlightenment and higher spiritual faculties, rests over the left hand, representing the world of maya, or illusion. (Carver n.d.)

This is just one of many hand mudras. Try it for 15 minutes and see how you feel. If you notice a calming or peaceful sensation, then make sure to add it to your list of coping strategies. Also make sure to look into other mudras you can try—these can be found online by searching for "hand mudra" and there are books on the topic.

Practice grounding

Grounding means bringing your attention to your surroundings through your senses. When you take a moment to intentionally notice what you see, hear, smell, feel, and taste, you bring yourself to the "here and now." Grounding is a coping skill that can be used when you are feeling overwhelmed with thoughts or feelings.

▶ 5,4,3,2,1 GROUNDING

5,4,3,2,1 Grounding is a simple and easy to remember technique. It entails thinking of five things you can see, four things you can hear, three things you can smell, two things you can feel, and one thing you can taste.

DIRECTIONS

- Close your eyes for a moment and take a few deep breaths.

- Look around you and take in the view and your surroundings. What is going on in front of you? Are any objects or people moving? What colors do you see you right now? Name five things you can see.

- Next, listen to the noises around you. If you are indoors, for instance, do you hear any people talking? Do you hear any appliances or music? If you are outdoors, do you hear birds singing? Do you hear traffic close or far away? Can you hear any wind blowing? Name four things you can hear.

- Then focus on what you can smell. Do you smell any cleaners, cigarette smoke, gum, car exhaust, candles, or fresh air? Name three things you can smell.

- Next, feel your body and any sensations it might be experiencing. Can you feel the texture of your clothing? Can you feel the weight of your head? Can you feel the ground beneath your feet? Are you feeling hungry or full? Name two things you can feel.

- Last, focus on your sense of taste. Name one thing you can taste.

- When you are done, take a moment to reflect on how it felt to tune in to your senses and be in the moment.

Use the "5,4,3,2,1 Grounding Exercise" worksheet to remind yourself of this method.

*

5,4,3,2,1 Grounding Exercise

· ·

5

Name 5 things you can see

4

Name 4 things you can hear

3

Name 3 things you can smell

2

Name 2 things you can feel

1

Name 1 thing you can taste

Do a body scan

Body scanning is a brief activity in which you quiet your body and mind so you can tune in to any messages your body might be trying to tell you. Body scans are especially helpful on busy days or at transition times (e.g. before you head out the door to school or work, when you are heading from one parent's house to another, or when you've been non-stop busy for more than a couple of hours).

▶ **BODY SCAN** ·

DIRECTIONS

- Take a moment to get comfortable.

- Close your eyes and turn your focus to your body.

- Start by bringing your attention to your feet and observe any sensations that might cue you to anything your feet need at the moment.

- Then move your attention to your shins, knees, upper legs, and so on, until you get to your head.

- At each area pause and "listen"—see if you can tell what your body wants you to know about each area.

- When you are done scanning your body, take a deep breath and, in your mind, say "thank you" to your body.

It's that easy!

When you are new to doing body scans you might be wondering what kind of "messages" your body might give you. Here are some examples:

- If your feet and legs are tired, perhaps you want warm clean socks, a foot soak, or cosy slippers. If your legs and feet have been still all day (e.g. sitting at a desk), maybe you want to get up and move about, take a walk, or walk barefoot outside. If you have achy muscles in your feet and legs, your body may cue you that it wants you to soak them in the tub, or to massage those sore muscles.

- Your belly might tell you that it's hungry. If it does, what does your body want you to eat? If you recently ate something, can you tell how your body is responding to that food?

- If you notice that your belly is feeling tight, nervous, or queasy, it might be your body's way of signaling an uncomfortable situation or person in your life, or that you are holding your feelings in rather than standing up for yourself.

- Similarly, your throat might feel tight if there is something you need to speak up about, or if you are holding back feelings. If your throat is feeling raw and hot, perhaps you're coming down with a cold, or maybe you've been arguing or yelling. Listen to what your throat is trying to tell you about what it needs— perhaps you need to speak your truth, or to quiet your voice and give someone else a chance to speak. Perhaps you need some TLC for your throat, like healing tea or to rest your vocal cords. Maybe your body wants you to do some vocal toning, singing, or chanting.

These are just a few of the many possible messages your body could be telling you. The more you practice body scanning and listening to what your body tells you, the quicker and easier it becomes. As you get better at listening to your body's cues the easier it will be to care for your needs.

Use distraction

There are times when distraction is a wonderful coping strategy. It's especially helpful for those who feel their feelings intensely and for those who have trouble making good choices when under stress. Here are times when teens and tweens like yourself have used distraction for a coping strategy:

"When my boyfriend broke up with me and all I wanted to do was to keep texting him, begging him to reconsider. Instead, I kept myself busy and got through it. It wasn't easy to do, but at least I didn't end up acting out in ways I knew I would regret later."

"I used distraction a lot after a death in my family. I was really sad and I couldn't handle feeling that level of sadness 24/7. I had to plan time each day to do something distracting to get a break from it. I was still really sad, but at least it gave my brain a chance to think about something else for a bit."

"I had a major surgery planned and I was really nervous about it. Each time I went into a new room at the hospital I would look for heart shapes—I found them in the ceiling tiles, in the floor patterns, and sometimes in things out the window, like leaves and clouds. It helped to focus on finding the hearts rather than panicking about the procedure."

"Instead of hurting myself or others I now have a bunch of things I use for distraction— sometimes I do push ups and sit ups, other times I shoot baskets, and sometimes I watch a movie."

Use the "Distraction Action Plan" worksheet to list the activities you will try or use when you need a distraction. The next time you need a distracting activity to do, you'll have plenty of ideas to choose from.

You can also use the following handouts to get ideas for your action plan:

- "Random Acts of Kindness and Gratitude"

- "Get Outdoors"

You can also refer to activities listed under the "Exercise and move your body" section and the "Play" section.

*

Distraction Action Plan

· ·

When I need a distraction I will try one or more of the following activities:

_____

_____

_____

_____

_____

_____

_____

_____

_____

_____

_____

_____

_____

_____

_____

_____

_____

_____

▶ GENERAL DISTRACTION ACTIVITIES

These simple activities can be added to your "Distraction Action Plan" if they interest you:

- Look through flip books.

- Look through a book or card deck about optical illusions.

- Do a picture puzzle, such as spot the difference or a rebus puzzle.

- Do word puzzles such as acrostics, word finds, crossword puzzles, or cryptograms.

- Do a math or logic puzzle such as logic problems, coding games, or math problems.

- Do a mechanical puzzle such as a jigsaw puzzle or hand-held puzzle such as a Rubik's™ Cube.

- Look through a Wonder Journal (see Create a Wonder Journal handout).

- Watch a funny movie.

- Look through a collection of yours.

- Find a sensory-rich activity to do such as: eat something super-spicy or cold, do an intense exercise, take a hot shower, or lay on an acupressure mat.

- Reorganize or clean your room.

- Read a book.

- Work on a project such as fixing up a bike, making a new piece of art, or writing new lyrics to a song.

▶ LOOK FOR HEARTS

Look for heart shapes in everyday objects—you might find them in the clouds, in a bowl of soup, in a cracked piece of concrete on the sidewalk, on the ceiling tile, in a fabric pattern, etc. See how many you can find in one area, in one day, or in a week. If you're able, photograph each heart you find to remind yourself of how many hearts are around you on any given day.

▶ NOTICE NATURE

Notice the beauty of nature that's around you. It could be the changing colors in the sky at sunset, a reflection in a puddle, a flower, a starlit sky, tree roots, the intricacy of a spider's web, or the leaves of a houseplant. Notice the unlikely places where nature takes hold, such as a crack in the sidewalk or moss growing between bricks on a building. Allow yourself to feel awe or curiosity as you notice what nature has to offer.

▶ LOOK FOR KINDNESS

Look for people being kind to others. It could be someone opening the door for someone else, a license plate or bumper sticker that has a positive message on it, a courteous note left for someone, a friendly smile from one person to another, a person carrying a bouquet of flowers, a thoughtful comment on someone's social media, a compliment someone gave you, etc. If you like, keep a journal documenting these acts of kindness from day to day. These moments can remind you that there are people in this world showing compassion, respect, and generosity to one another. I especially like this intervention for times when the news is saturated with stories of violence, oppression, and cruelty.

▶ FIND FACES IN EVERYDAY OBJECTS

"Pareidolia" is when you see faces in everyday objects. You might be able to find faces in the following objects: the exterior of houses (sometimes the windows look like eyes and the door looks like a mouth), electrical outlets, car bumpers, or even your food. Look around and see how many faces you can find in a week. Photograph the ones you find and keep a collection of them.

Get outside in nature

Fresh air, sunshine, and nature are wonderful antidotes to daily stress. In fact, there are many scientific reasons why nature is good for our mental health, including the following:

> You've probably learned by now that we can get vitamin D from sunshine. But did you know that vitamin D also has an impact on our moods? That's because vitamin D is important for regulating neurotransmitters in our bodies, the same neurotransmitters than can make us feel depressed. (Greenblatt 2011)

Too little vitamin D can lead to seasonal affective disorder and depression, so it's important to get healthy amounts of vitamin D—both from sunshine and from your diet. Neurotransmitters are chemicals in your body that help your nerve cells (also called neurons) communicate to each other. Soil is another place we get support for our neurotransmitters:

> Mycobacterium vaccae is the substance under study and has indeed been found to mirror the effect on neurons that drugs like Prozac provide. The bacterium is found in soil and may stimulate serotonin production, which makes you relaxed and happier. Studies were conducted on cancer patients and they reported a better quality of life and less stress. Lack of serotonin has been linked to depression, anxiety, obsessive compulsive disorder and bipolar problems. The bacterium appears to be a natural antidepressant in

soil and has no adverse health effects. These antidepressant microbes in soil may be as easy to use as just playing in the dirt. (Grant n.d.)

Just walking outdoors in a natural setting can lift your mood too:

A new study finds quantifiable evidence that walking in nature could lead to a lower risk of depression. Specifically, the study, published in *Proceedings of the National Academy of Science*, found that people who walked for 90 minutes in a natural area, as opposed to participants who walked in a high-traffic urban setting, showed decreased activity in a region of the brain associated with a key factor in depression. (Jordan 2015)

I am so passionate about the benefits of nature on our mental health that I even wrote an entire book on it called *How to Get Kids Offline, Outdoors, and Connecting to Nature: 200+ Creative Activities to Encourage Self-Esteem, Mindfulness, and Wellbeing*. Getting outdoors in nature truly improves wellbeing. See the handout "Get Outdoors" for ideas of things to do.

USING NATURE TO CALM

Niki Willows[2]

When I feel anxious or cross I sometimes need to take myself away from wherever I am. I like to go outside and either walk or just sit and watch things for a while. It gives me time to clear my head, zone out and sort out my thoughts. If I'm angry I find that walking very, VERY fast is an effective way to pace it out. I like to go and find a green space or a blue space outside. A green space is somewhere that I can see some trees or if I'm in a city maybe a park with some grass or flowers, or a garden. If I'm at home I live by the sea and my blue space is watching the waves. Sometimes the sky is also my blue space, and I lie to lie on my back and watch the clouds. You can even do this from inside a building.

I find a rock, a bench or a dry bit of sand (depends where I am!) and sit and watch the clouds, sea or trees move. I try hard to tune out thoughts whizzing round my head and concentrate on the movement of the waves etc. Then slowly I tune in my ears to the sound of the waves or the wind. I listen carefully and watch. It's not always easy. Sometimes thoughts will just keep popping up in my head and I tell them to go away and concentrate on the natural things that I'm looking at. After a while I can feel myself calming down and usually things don't seem quite so bad. Once I'm calm I think about what made me feel that way and what I can do about it. Sometimes things happen that you can't do much about but maybe you can react to it differently the next time.

2 Niki has an education in Forest Schools, Early Years, children with complex needs and play development. She runs family stay and play sessions in and around Porthtowan, Cornwall as well as the Firestarters After School Club. She has a licence from Cornwall Council to run Beach Teach and Play sessions on Porthtowan beach. She created the Inspirational Outdoors Conference with Martin Besford from Highway Farm Activity Centre.

*

Get Outdoors

· ·

Take a walk with a friend, your dog, and/or a loved one.

Sit outside while you do your homework or chat with friends.

Play basketball.

Eat your next meal outdoors.

Go on a picnic with friends—try various locations like local parks, backyards, fire escapes, terraces/decks, along a trail.

Visit a local arboretum.

Explore a local trail with friends.

Go letter boxing or geocaching.

Find your way through an outdoor maze (e.g. a corn maze in autumn).

Watch the sunset.

Create a fun snow sculpture.

Have a snowball fight.

Go sledding—find creative ways to sled down a grassy hill, a snowy hill, or even a sandy hill.

Collect natural materials for a nature-based craft.

Take a night walk in your neighborhood with friends or family.

Join a beach clean, trail clean-up, or other outdoor volunteer group.

Visit a local park to read a book, catch up with friends, or do homework.

If you live in a high-rise with roof access, consider planting container gardens on the roof.

Go to a drive-in movie and sit in on a blanket or in the back of a car with the windows all open.

Go camping, even if it's in your yard.

Pick flowers.

Play a game outside.

Climb a tree.

Visit a local farm or orchard.

Go for a swim.

Watch a meteor shower—look online for when meteor showers are scheduled to happen in your area.

Get up early to watch the sunrise.

Decorate a paved area with chalk.

Join a community garden and grow some of your own foods.

Add LED lights to a kite and fly it at night.

Create land art—e.g. write inspiring words with natural materials outdoors, such as "PEACE" spelled out with sticks or acorns; make a dandelion chain and hang it on a chain link fence for decoration; make a spiral shape in the sand or dirt, etc.

▶ EARTHING AND GROUNDING

"Earthing" (sometimes called "grounding") is the term used for connecting your body to the earth, e.g. walking barefoot, sitting on the ground, or swimming in natural water. "Grounding" is a term used for earthing in addition to the use of other interventions that create the same effects as earthing, e.g. using grounded products. Earthing and grounding are terms that are often used interchangeably. Earthing and grounding can have a positive impact on your wellbeing by calming your mind and body, but also by reducing inflammation, and more:

> Grounding appears to improve sleep, normalize the day–night cortisol rhythm, reduce pain, reduce stress, shift the autonomic nervous system from sympathetic toward parasympathetic activation, increase heart rate variability, speed wound healing, and reduce blood viscosity. A summary has been published in the *Journal of Environmental and Public Health*. (Oschman, Chevalier, and Brown 2015)

> From a practical standpoint, clinicians could recommend outdoor 'barefoot sessions' to patients, weather, and conditions permitting. Ober *et al.* have observed that going barefoot as little as 30 or 40 minutes daily can significantly reduce pain and stress. (Chevalier *et al.* 2012)

You can practice earthing and grounding by doing the following:

- Sit on the ground under a tree.

- Swim in the ocean, a pond, or a lake.

- Walk barefoot on the beach, in the woods, or anywhere outdoors (be mindful of where you step—avoid stepping on unsafe or unsanitary objects as you walk).

- Lay in the grass or on a large rock.

- Sit on a concrete surface outside.

Earthing methods tend to be recommended for about 30–40 minutes at a time.

▶ FOREST BATHING

Forest bathing refers to spending time in the forest, among trees and greenery, while taking in all the smells, sights, colors, and textures of the surroundings:

> A 15-minute walk in the woods causes measurable changes in physiology. Japanese researchers led by Yoshifumi Miyazaki at Chiba University sent 84 subjects to stroll in seven different forests, while the same number of volunteers walked around city centers. The forest walkers hit a relaxation jackpot: Overall they showed a 16 percent decrease in the stress hormone cortisol, a 2 percent drop in blood pressure, and a 4 percent drop in heart rate. Miyazaki believes our bodies relax in pleasant, natural surroundings because they evolved there. Our senses are adapted to interpret information about plants and streams, he says, not traffic and high-rises. (Williams n.d.)

> Numerous studies show that both exercising in forests and simply sitting looking at trees reduce blood pressure as well as the stress-related hormones cortisol and adrenaline. Looking at pictures of trees has a similar, but less dramatic, effect. Studies examining the same activities in urban, unplanted areas showed no reduction of stress-related effects. Using the Profile of Mood States test, researchers found that forest bathing trips significantly decreased the scores for anxiety, depression, anger, confusion and fatigue. And because stress inhibits the immune system, the stress-reduction benefits of forests are further magnified. (Department of Environmental Conservation n.d.)

If you'd like to try forest bathing for yourself, but are not sure where your nearest forest is, use an online search engine to locate the closest local park, public garden, botanical garden, or arboretum.

Burn off adrenaline

A major role of adrenaline is to prepare your body for a life-threatening event or significant stress. For example, if you crossed the road and a distracted driver started driving toward you, your body—in a split second—would release adrenaline to prepare you to run fast out of the way. When you get a surge of adrenaline your heart beats faster, you start sweating, and the blood in your body goes to major organs like your heart (which means blood goes away from your digestive organs—this is one reason people get stomach aches or nausea when anxious). Adrenaline is helpful in life-threatening events. But some people's bodies release adrenaline under small amounts of stress or even no stress at all. This is why anxiety feels so terrible—your body is acting like a life-threatening event is happening when it's not.

Adrenaline and anxiety often go hand in hand because when you become anxious, your body releases adrenaline. The good news, however, is there is a way to burn off that adrenaline—with cardiovascular exercise. The next time you feel anxious, do an exercise that gets your heart pumping and aim for 30 minutes of aerobic activity.

If you experience anxiety often, start doing 30 minutes of cardiovascular activity a day.

Check in with a doctor or provider if you have questions or concerns about starting a new exercise routine.

Release tension

When people feel stressed they tend to tense up their muscles and hold their breath. Have you noticed that before with your own body? Do you have certain muscles that seem tighter when you're under stress? Try the following activities for ways to release that tension and relax those muscles.

▶ PROGRESSIVE MUSCLE RELAXATION

Progressive muscle relaxation is a technique where you tense up different muscle groups on purpose and then release the tension. It's a great intervention for relaxing your whole body, not just one area.

DIRECTIONS

- Find a relaxing place to sit or lay down.

- Get comfortable and take a few deep breaths.

- Tense up the muscles in your feet.

- Hold that tension in your feet for the count of ten, and then let go of the tension.

- Visualize a wave of relaxation flowing through your feet.

- Next, tense up the muscles in your calves.

- Hold the tension in your calves for a count of ten, and then release the tension.

- Again, visualize a wave of relaxation flowing through your calves.

- Keep repeating this pattern as you move upwards through your body, addressing the thighs and buttocks, stomach, hands, arms, back and shoulders, and finally, your face.

- When you've tensed and released all the areas of your body, sit or lie quietly, and allow your body to feel the relaxation.

▶ ISOMETRIC EXERCISES

Isometric exercises are when you contract certain muscles without moving them. Since there is no motion involved, it's a good calming strategy for the classroom—no one will know you are using these exercises. I work with some youth who use these for calming (through the release of tension) and others who use it for managing anxiety (through burning off some adrenaline). Try one or both of these isometric exercises and see how they feel for you.

- One isometric exercise you can try is pressing your palms together: Place your hands together, palm to palm and finger to finger. Take a breath in and hold it while you simultaneously press your palms together. Hold your breath and press your palms for the count of five. Then let go and exhale.

- Another exercise you can try is pressing your ankles together. Sit with your ankles crossed. Then inhale, hold that breath, and press your ankles together for a count of five. Release and exhale.

There are more isometric exercises to try, but these two are the most used by the youth I work with.

▶ SQUISH AND SQUEEZE

Squish and squeeze is similar to isometric exercises because you use muscle contraction for tension release. In this case, however, you have an external object to work with, such as a stress ball. A stress ball is a great example of something you can squish and squeeze. Other items you can use are clay, bread dough, Play-Doh, and hand exercisers. Any of these items can be used to squish and squeeze when you need to release tension in your hands or body. These are also helpful items to have around (e.g. in your backpack or the glove compartment of a car) and/or add to a Calming Kit (see Self-Care Kits handout).

▶ PUT YOUR FEET UP A WALL

This is one of my favorite calming strategies for releasing tension. It's quite simple too—lie on your back on the floor (or your bed) and put your feet up against the wall. It works best when you scoot your bottom as close to the wall as you comfortably can. Then lay your arms on the floor (or bed) and let your body rest quietly for 10–15 minutes. See if—or when—you notice the tension in your body letting go and when your mind starts to quiet.

As with any strategy, if you feel dizzy or uncomfortable at any time, stop what you're doing.

Take a break

When stress levels are high or feelings are intense, it's an opportune time to take a break. Whether it's homework, an argument, or another stress-inducing event, take a few minutes to step away and use your coping skills. For instance, take a brisk walk, get a drink of water, use some of the strategies in this book, or talk to a friend. When you step away and take a break, you give your brain and body a chance to recalibrate and return to the task at hand, feeling more focused and centered.

Use aromatherapy

Aromatherapy is the use of essential oils to help with a variety of conditions. It is commonly used for its relaxation and calming effects.

The aromatherapy interventions listed in this book are widely used and considered to be safe. However, if you have allergies to any of the herbs, flowers, or plants used in aromatherapy, do not use them.

▶ **CALMING LAVENDER SPRAY**

Lavender flowers and essential oil are regularly used for calming the mind and body. You might be familiar with this fragrance already, since it is found in many bath and body products, cleaning products, and sprays. You can make your own calming lavender spray using lavender essential oil. When you want or need some calming aromatherapy, you can spray this in the air where you are.

Note: Be mindful about spraying anything around others without asking them first. Some people are sensitive and reactive to fragrances.

MATERIALS

Isopropyl ("rubbing") alcohol or witch hazel

Lavender essential oil

Distilled or filtered water

A 2 oz. glass spray/spritzer bottle (can be purchased at your local health food store or pharmacy)

DIRECTIONS

- Place two teaspoons of the isopropyl alcohol or witch hazel in your 2 oz. spritzer bottle.

- Add ten drops of the lavender essential oil.

- Fill the remainder of the bottle with the distilled or filtered water.

- Shake the bottle.

- Try a test spray. If you want a stronger lavender scent, then add up to five more drops and shake it again.

- Spritz the lavender spray in the air around you, whenever you want some calming aromatherapy.

▶ FOCUS SPRAY

A focus spray is helpful when you need to pay attention to something such as reading or studying. The spray uses the essential oils from peppermint and rosemary that have invigorating and awakening properties to them.

MATERIALS

Isopropyl ("rubbing") alcohol or witch hazel

Peppermint essential oil

Rosemary essential oil

Distilled or filtered water

A 2 oz. glass spray/spritzer bottle (can be purchased at your local health food store or pharmacy)

DIRECTIONS

- Place two teaspoons of the isopropyl alcohol or witch hazel in your 2 oz. spritzer bottle.

- Add five drops of the peppermint essential oil.

- Add ten drops of the rosemary oil.

- Fill the remainder of the bottle with the distilled or filtered water.

- Shake the bottle.

- Spray in the air around you as needed, when you need a little help with focus and concentration.

Have a calming bath

Baths can be a calming intervention. For many people there is nothing quite like a warm soak in the bathtub to wind down after a stressful day. Candlelight, bath lights, glow sticks (unopened), bubbles, bubble bath, bathing salts, or flower petals can be added to your bath to make the experience even more relaxing or enjoyable. If you do not have access to a bathtub, consider using foot baths instead. Small tubs can be used to soak your feet and you will still get the relaxing benefits.

▶ FLOWER AND HERBAL BATHS

Flower and herbal baths can be aromatic, beautiful, and healing. There are key points to remember, however, when having a flower or herbal bath:

- Make sure you are not allergic to any of the flowers or herbs you put in your bathtub. This may sound like common sense; however, many flowers and herbs come from "families" that you need to be aware of. For example, if you are allergic to ragweed, then do not use chamomile in your bathwater because it is a relative to ragweed (Brody 1995).

- Only use flowers and herbs that are organic and that have not been sprayed with chemicals.

- When using flowers, use only the blossoms or petals.

- Look online for native flowers in your area that can be safely added to baths. Roses and lavender are pretty common for bath use and can be bought in dried form if necessary. Geranium leaves, jasmine, and yarrow can also be used (Kirkland 1992).

Herbal baths can also be made using cotton muslin bags, "bath tea" bags, large tea balls, or even cheesecloth to contain the herbs. "Herbal baths" sometimes refer to a broader term for baths in which you combine flowers, herbs, oils, and salts. You can use the flowers mentioned above, as well as red clover buds, oatmeal, peppermint leaf, eucalyptus, calendula, chamomile, passionflower, and holy basil leaf (Mountain Rose Herbs 2016).

▶ MINERAL SALT BATHS

Epsom salts can be added to your bath to help ease muscle aches and pains. Purchase plain Epsom salts without added fragrances and follow the directions on the package for the recommended amount to add to your bath.

▶ FOOT BATHS

If you do not have access to a bathtub, foot baths are the next best thing. Soaking your feet in a small portable tub is not only relaxing, but it also conserves water and is less expensive. You can add flowers, herbs, and mineral salts to your foot baths just as you would for regular baths, and you won't need as many materials since you're filling a small tub versus a large one.

To prepare for a foot bath, make sure you have towels available—one to go underneath the small tub (in case of dripping and spills) and one next to you to dry your feet after the bath.

Use fidgets

"Fidgets" are items you hold in your hands. Oftentimes (but not always) they have movable parts. Some people use fidgets to help increase their focus or to reduce anxious energy. They can be soothing for people who need sensory input, thereby helping them focus and calm more easily.

There are many types of fidgets you can buy, but you can also make your own. Making your own is usually more cost effective and they are easier to replace if broken or lost.

▶ FIDGET SPINNERS

Assembling a fidget spinner is a fairly easy process, but if you don't have skateboard bearings and metal bonding glue, you will need to purchase these ahead of time. Skateboard bearings tend to be packaged in multiples of four, which is convenient since it takes four bearings to make one spinner.

MATERIALS

4 skateboard bearings

Dish soap

A small bottle brush

Metal-bonding glue

Permanent ink marker (optional)

Zip ties (optional)

DIRECTIONS

- Before you start you will want to remove the metal cap from one of the bearings. This will be your center bearing. By removing the cap you reduce friction and allow your spinner to spin longer and more smoothly. To remove the cap take a strong edge (such as a butter knife) and gently pry it under the cap of the bearing. The cap should come off easily.

- The bearing will have an oil lubricant inside and you'll need to wash this out. You can soak the bearing in soapy hot water, and then use a small bottle brush to scrub the lubricant off. You may need to repeat this step until all the lubricant has been removed.

- Make sure this bearing is completely dry before moving on to the next step.

- Place this bearing on a flat surface.

- Align the other three bearings so they are evenly spaced apart from each other on the outside of the center bearing.

- If helpful, make a small tic mark on each bearing to show where your bearings will be placed. This will help you to keep track of the placement of the bearings when you're gluing.

- One bearing at a time, apply your glue to the contact point where it touches the center bearing. Repeat for all three bearings.

- Wait for the glue to cure.

- An optional step at this point is to add a zip tie around the outer bearings for extra structural integrity, allowing your spinner to survive a few falls.

▶ FIDGETS ON THE GO

You can make or collect a variety of fidgets that are inexpensive, wearable, and portable (e.g. they fit in a pocket). The easiest pocket versions are those that are small objects. For example, a clean bottle cap, a button, a marble, a paper clip, or a coin can be placed in your pocket for times when you're feeling unfocused or need to bring your attention to the moment. Bring the item out of your pocket whenever you need something to fidget with for these purposes.

Textured fabric can also be sewn into the inside (or end) of a sleeve or on the bottom hem of a shirt. Velcro, velour, and corduroy are examples of textured fabrics. When you feel the urge to fidget, you can run your fingers over the different textured areas.

▶ WASHER NECKLACES

Washer necklaces are easy to make and the washers are satisfying to fidget with. They can be worn, which makes them portable and user-friendly. However, do not shower, swim, or sleep with your washer necklace on.

MATERIALS

A stainless steel washer sized 1.5" to 2" diameter (if you don't have spare ones at your house, you can buy them at the hardware store)

Nail polish

String, bakers twine, or suede necklace cord

Large bead (optional)

Plate, pan, or parchment paper where the washers can dry after painting them

DIRECTIONS

- Use fingernail polish to paint one side of a washer. A thick layer is recommended.

- Allow the washer to dry.

- Repeat for the opposite side of the washer. You can choose a different color nail polish if you like.

- Measure out a length of string for your necklace that will allow for two knots and easily fit over your head.

- Attach your string or cord to the washer. Fold the string in half, pull the rounded end through the center of the washer, then pull the loose ends of the necklace through the loop you created. This should secure the washer to the necklace. Tug on the knot to tighten it.

- If you'd like to add a large bead, hold the two necklace ends together and slip a bead over them. The bead will now sit on top of the washer.

- Tie a knot with the necklace ends, and make sure it's secure before trimming the ends.

- Slip the necklace over your head. Anytime you need an item to fidget with, you can now do so with your necklace.

CREATIVE COPING SKILLS FOR TEENS AND TWEENS

Listen to music

Music can be motivating, energizing, uplifting, and transcendent. It can also be calming, meditative, and emotive. People have enjoyed these therapeutic effects of music and rhythm for as long as they've been around.

What music do you listen to when you've had a bad day or when you're angry? What do you listen to when you need to study or do homework? What music do you listen to when you want to fall asleep, relax, or meditate? How does music impact your life overall?

Read the excerpt written by counselor Rachel Wells for some music therapy activities that integrate music with coping strategies.

MUSIC THERAPY ACTIVITIES

Rachel Wells, LCPC, MMT, MT-BC

Identifying music for relaxation

Goal and purpose: The purpose of finding music to help us relax is exactly what it sounds like! When we are feeling anxious, stressed out, or are needing to focus, we need to bring our bodies back to a calm, composed state. When we are able to relax our bodies, the stress hormones decrease, allowing us to think more clearly, breathe more deeply, and release physical tension.

Materials needed: Your favorite online music streaming application or music collection.

Time requirements: 15 minutes to one hour.

Step-by-step description of activity: For this activity, there is no clear step-by-step process. Since each person finds relaxation music to be unique, this is something you will need to explore on your own. Typically, most people find relaxation music to be 60 beats per minute or slower in regards to tempo (the pace of the music). An easy way to determine the speed is to picture yourself walking through a park. The music should be the speed of walking slowly. If you're jogging, it's probably too much! Additionally, instrumental music is also generally preferred to songs with lyrics.

The list below is just a few genres of music that you can search the internet for:

- Ocean sounds

- Nature sounds

- Instrumental folk, guitar, or piano

- Slow jazz

- Slow instrumental R&B

- Native American flute

- "Largo" section of classical music

- Easy listening

- New Age

- Ambient

Once you have exhausted your search, create a playlist of the ones you like best. The next time you begin to feel stressed or anxious, you can reach for this playlist to help calm your body and bring you to a more relaxed state.

Prompted rapping

Goal and purpose: The primary goal of prompted rapping is to allow ourselves to "let go" and allow whatever wants to come out of our mouths to do so. Rapping, especially freestyle, is a difficult skill and takes practice, but it can be much easier if you start with prompts and a framework. An additional purpose of rapping is to have fun and express yourself!

Materials needed:

- Your voice

- Rap beat loops (you can find them easily by searching for instrumental rap beats on your internet search engine or app store)

- Pen and paper/index cards

- Rhyming dictionary or search engine

Time requirements: 30–60 minutes.

Step-by-step description of activity: Begin by creating cards that have three to four words that rhyme on them. I like to have at least five different cards to choose from. In general, these words should loosely connect to each other in some way. Next, search the internet for instrumental rap beat loops and select one that you would like to use. For this next step, you can either freestyle using the card you selected and simply see what comes out, or, you can compose ahead of time what you would like to say before trying to sing it. This is a good way for those who have never rapped and may be a little hesitant to try. For example, the card I choose may look something like this:

> Outrage
> Disengage
> Caged

If I choose to write my rap before singing it, it may look something like this:

> Whenever she speaks I feel outrage,
> I don't know what to do so I disengage,
> By holding it in I feel so caged.

Some things to consider after the activity:

- What was it like to try prompted rapping?

- Did you say anything that surprised you?

- Was it easier or harder than you thought?

- How can you adapt this activity to fit your needs?

Lyric trading cards

Goal and purpose: The goal of this activity is to create miniature art that we can keep with us as little reminders of messages we may need to hear. This activity is great to use as a group or with friends and family, because, as the title implies, they are fun to trade!

Materials needed:

- Cardstock cut into 2" x 3" rectangles

- Art supplies, such as crayons, markers, magazines, glue, etc.

- Lyrics of a song you find meaning in

Time requirements: 15–30 minutes.

Step-by-step description of activity: Begin by choosing a lyric that you find inspirational or that has a message that resonates with you, and write the lyric on the card. Once you have written the lyric, begin to decorate your card. Lastly, trade your card or keep it in a pocket for days when you need a little inspiration.

Some suggestions for decorating:

- Print the lyrics by cutting out the letters from a magazine and gluing them onto the paper.

- Glue two cards together by only gluing one edge, creating a card/book to secretly place the lyric inside.

- Print the lyrics and glue onto the paper (if you prefer computer fonts over handwriting).

- Print out or use a photo as the card, and then place the lyric over the photo.

- Give the card some volume! Adding a ribbon or gem can make it more three-dimensional.

Use visualization

Visualization is when you use your imagination to mentally prepare for something. For example, if you had a presentation that you had to give in front of the class, you could mentally rehearse it in your mind prior to doing it. Visualization can help reduce anxiety about an event by being better prepared for it:

> According to research using brain imagery, visualization works because neurons in our brains, those electrically excitable cells that transmit information, interpret imagery as equivalent to a real-life action. When we visualize an act, the brain generates an impulse that tells our neurons to 'perform' the movement. This creates a new neural pathway—clusters of cells in our brain that work together to create memories or learned behaviors—that primes our body to act in a way consistent to what we imagined. All of this occurs without actually performing the physical activity, yet it achieves a similar result. (Niles 2011)

When you use visualization, include imagery of what will happen just prior to the event itself to give you some added preparation. If we use the class presentation as an example, this is how it might sound in your mind as you visually rehearse each step of the process:

> I will go to my locker before class in order to get my presentation materials. When I open my locker I will look in the mirror on the inside of my locker door to make sure I look ready for the presentation. I will gather my presentation supplies from my locker and head to the classroom. I will put my materials on the table where the teacher told us we could. I will sit at my desk and take a few deep breaths. I'm presenting second,

so I will listen to the first presentation. I will continue to take deep breaths as needed. I will tell myself that the presentation only lasts ten minutes and that I'm prepared and ready to do this. When it's my turn, the teacher will call on me. I will go to the table and collect my presentation materials to set them up on the table in front of the class. I will then start my presentation. I will say...

When you create a script for your visualization, continue through to the very end of the event. Each time you go over the script in your mind, your brain will be more prepared to succeed. You do not need to write a script down—you can just imagine each step in natural succession.

Teens especially have a lot to prepare for, so visualization is a valuable skill to learn. The next time you have a job interview, a driving test, a college interview, or if you want to ask someone special to the prom, mentally rehearse it prior to doing so.

Create art

Art is a venue for relaxation and it can be added to your "toolkit" for calming strategies. Even if you believe you're not good at it, 45 minutes of creating art can reduce your stress and cortisol levels (Frank 2016). Creating art comes naturally for some, but for those of you who need some inspiration or specific ideas of how to make art, the following activities will get you started.

▶ COLORING AND ACTIVITY BOOKS

One of the easiest means of creating art is coloring, typically done in coloring books or pages. Coloring books vary in difficulty and topic, so regardless of your interests, you are likely to find a coloring book with a theme you like. Coloring pages can also be downloaded and printed from a computer. You can color pictures using a variety of mediums including markers, ink pens, colored pencils, watercolor pencils, or crayons.

Activity books tend to offer more variety of coloring options such as "color by number," pixelated coloring activities, or "extreme coloring."

If you feel like you have absolutely no artistic drive whatsoever, and/or you just don't know where to start, the color by number coloring pages are a perfect place to begin. These are pictures that tell you what to color and where to color it. It takes no thought, and you can just dive right in and lose yourself in the calming activity of coloring.

▶ WATERCOLOR SQUARES

MATERIALS

Paper

Watercolor paints

Paint brush

Black permanent ink pen

DIRECTIONS

- Use your permanent ink pen to draw a few rows of squares. Paint each square a slightly different shade from the one next to it. To create various shades you can either add more or less water to your paint or add a different color to your paint, a small amount at a time.

- When your painting has dried, notice how the colors evolve from one painted square to the next.

▶ JOURNALING WITH WATERCOLOR SQUARES

Journaling with watercolor squares is an activity for tracking your moods and feelings during a specific period of time. It can be done as a single sit-down activity in which you reflect back on a period of time (e.g. if you want to journal about your day or week), or you can choose to paint a square each day throughout a week or month.

MATERIALS

Paper

Watercolor paints

Paint brush

Black permanent ink pen

DIRECTIONS

- Draw squares on a piece of paper and then fill the squares with watercolor paint using colors that represent how you feel or felt at a certain time. You can choose a number of squares to represent the hours in a day (e.g. 24 squares, each representing an hour on the clock), days in the week (seven squares), or days in the month (28–31 squares).

- Use your black ink pen to draw several squares on a piece of paper. Make sure the pen is permanent ink, otherwise the ink will "bleed" once you add paint.

- Choose or create a color using watercolor paints that represent your mood or feeling at that time. For example, one square might be a cheerful color to represent how happy you were it was the weekend, and another square might be dark and gloomy to represent the fight you had with a friend.

- If you keep track of your moods and feelings using watercolor squares, you may notice patterns emerging. For example, if you try this activity for several days, you might find that certain days of the week or hours of the day tend to be gloomier than others. If you notice any patterns, plan for extra self care during those times if needed.

▶ DOODLING VIA SHAPE REPETITION

Doodling is another activity that allows the mind to quiet and focus. Some people are natural doodlers—they can fill pages with random doodles and/or turn their school notes and other pages into works of art. On the flip side, there are many people who have no idea how to doodle. Shape repetition is a middle ground for everyone. Shape repetition merely means you choose one shape and you repeatedly draw it on paper. It's an easy way to doodle.

For example, fill a page, half a page, or just a corner of the page with circles. You can choose different-sized circles or all the same-sized circles. The circles can overlap, or not.

You can also draw many different triangles. The triangles can be of any size, they can intersect, or they can be separate. Other shapes to try include squares, diamonds, ovals, pentagons, or trapezoids. If you want to free hand your own kind of shapes, you can do that also! However you fill the page with your one shape is fine.

Once the shapes are drawn you can leave them as they are, or you can color the shapes in. You can also choose to color in the space between the shapes, leaving the shapes the color of the paper.

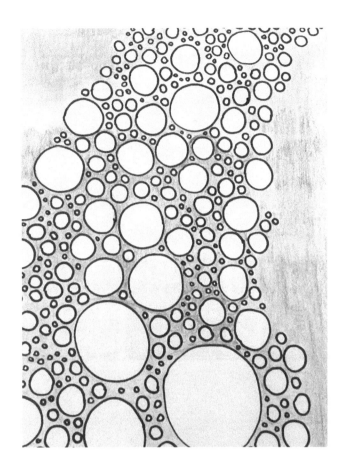

▶ CONCENTRIC CIRCLES

This activity is rather simple but it provides an uncomplicated means for creating art. You will only need paper and a pencil, although you can choose any drawing instrument.

DIRECTIONS

- Draw a dot in the center of your paper.

- Draw a circle around the dot, making sure (as much as possible) to make an even circle around the dot.

- Draw another circle around the one you just drew.

- Repeat until the entire page is filled with these "concentric circles," circles within circles.

▶ COLORING AND CREATING MANDALAS

In modern terms, a mandala is a circular picture that is often symmetrical and contains designs, patterns, and symbols. There are many mandala coloring books available for purchase, although if you have access to the internet and a printer, you can use your internet browser to search for "free mandala coloring pages" and print out what you need. These coloring books and pages are nice to have on hand for moments when you need a few minutes to calm or refocus.

If you are seeking an artistic challenge, however, you can try drawing your own mandalas "free hand," which means without any special tools or instruments.

MATERIALS

Paper

Pencil

Black marker or ink pen

Round objects to trace

A straight edge

DIRECTIONS

• Start with a pencil. Once you have a template for your mandala drawn, you can choose to switch over to an ink pen or marker pen.

• Choose an object in the room that is round on the bottom—e.g. a pencil holder, a drinking glass, a mug, or a food container. Make sure the bottom of whatever you choose is circular.

• Trace the circular shape on the paper using a pencil.

• Use a straight edge from a book, ruler, or other object to draw a straight line down the center of the circle. If you do not have a precise eye, you can pencil the line in lightly. Erase and create a new line if needed.

• Turn the circle and create an intersecting line down the middle again—this will create four semi-equal sections.

• Repeat the previous two steps if you would like your circle in eight semi-equal sections.

- If it helps, find smaller circular items to trace concentric circles in your mandala. This will help you to stay on track with more evenly spaced sections, but it isn't a necessity.

- Now add a shape or design in the center of the mandala, such as a square or a pattern.

- Add the next line of design—you can start a new pattern, or build off the one you just created.

- Continue filling in your mandala one layer at a time, until it's done.

- If you create a framework for a mandala that you really enjoy (or spent a lot of time creating), photocopy it before you draw in it. This way you will have a template for it.

- Another version of this activity is to free hand draw a mandala on black paper using white gel pen. Start with a dot in the center of your page and draw another circle or design around the dot. Continue to add layers of design and patterns around that dot until you create a mandala.

Mandala Template

MANDALA

Color this mandala and/or design your own.

▶ BODY POETRY AND ART

Body poetry and art is a creative experience in using your own body as an art medium. It's an experience that allows you to express yourself using written word, pictures, symbols, or designs.

MATERIALS

Temporary tattoo markers (but do not use if you are allergic to any of the ingredients in the markers)

Favorite poetry and quotes (written by you or by someone else)

DIRECTIONS

- Write poetry on your arms, legs, hands, or body using tattoo markers. You can choose poetry and quotes that inspire you, describe you, or express something you've been wanting to say to the world.

- You can also draw symbols, patterns, and designs on your skin with tattoo markers. If you need inspiration, look at preexisting tattoo or henna designs (e.g. from a book or online source), or use common everyday symbols such as stars, rainbows, peace signs, etc.

- Other ideas:

  — Draw hearts on areas of your body that you typically complain about or dislike.

  — Draw hearts, or another symbol of love and healing, on areas of your body where you have been hurt.

  — Write positive messages, such as "thank you," on parts of your body that need your love or acceptance.

▶ COLORING WITH PATTERNS

When we color pictures with markers or crayons, we typically fill in the sections of the picture with color. In this activity, however, you replace color with various patterns instead. For example, if you are coloring a picture of a flower, the flower will have many blossoms. Instead of coloring the blossoms, each one is filled in with a different pattern. One blossom might be "colored in" using thin vertical lines, the next might be filled in with small heart shapes, the next blossom might be "colored in" with zig zag lines, and so on.

A slightly different version of this activity is to write out a word in block letters or bubble letters and decorate each letter of the word using a different pattern. That word could be your name (or someone else's name) or it could be a word that calms you or motivates you. Sample words to write in bubble letters:

DREAM, CALM, HEAL, PLAY, LAUGH, PERSEVERE, RELAX, INSPIRE, BELIEVE, BREATHE, MOTIVATE, EXPLORE, SPARKLE, PEACE, DISCOVER, LOVE, HOPE, JOY, IMAGINE, MAGIC, BEAUTY, SHINE, COURAGE

Coloring In Template

Rather than coloring these flowers with color, try filling the spaces with different patterns instead.

▶ WAX AND WATERCOLOR PICTURES

This simple drawing activity allows for free form creating using wax and watercolor. You don't need any artistic talent or know-how to do this activity, which makes it perfect for new artists.

MATERIALS

White construction paper

Crayons or oil pastels

Watercolor paints (and water)

Tray or paper plate (if using liquid watercolor paint from tubes)

Paint brushes

DIRECTIONS

- Draw any design or picture on your paper using the crayons or oil pastels. Those who need ideas can try one or more of the following: draw a grid and color in the different squares; draw circles all over the page; scribble all over the page; draw waves; make random lines on the paper in any direction and of any size; write a word on the page, such as "PEACE"; or color the entire page using one or more colors.

- Prepare your watercolor paint. If you are using a watercolor tray (in which the watercolor is solid), add drops of water to each color to make your paint. If you are using tubes of watercolor paints, dab a small amount of paint on a paper plate and mix it with drops of water until the paint is the consistency and color you want.

- Dip a paint brush in the watercolor paint and then brush it across your picture. The paint will only absorb in areas where you have not used crayons or oil pastels.

- Allow your picture to dry.

▶ PATTERNED HAND

This activity is quite simple in that you trace your hand and then fill in the outline with one or more patterns. This project can be done with white or metallic ink pens on black paper, or with pencils and marker on white paper.

▶ THE EYES HAVE IT

I've noticed that when teens and tweens are invited to doodle or free draw in my office, eyes are a common subject to draw.

Here are some creative prompts based on drawing eyes:

- If these eyes belonged to _____, how do you think they see you? Draw yourself in the reflection of their eye the way you think they view you. You can choose a physical representation (e.g. how you think they view your physical self) or you can choose a metaphorical representation. Consider how any of the following people might view you differently—parents, a best friend, a romantic partner/significant other, an ex-partner, a teacher, a coach, society as a whole, a child, an adult, a stranger.

- Draw your own eyes or a representation of your eyes. Draw a reflection in your eyes of how you view a situation, a person, or a place. If you like, you can draw the true physical representation of it in one eye, and then how you personally view it in the other eye. For example, if you drew a picture of your childhood home, you could draw the actual structure reflected in one of the eyes (e.g. a house, a flat, a camper, etc.) and then draw how you perceived it in the other eye (e.g. a circus, a safe haven, a prison, an enchanted forest).

- Draw how you view yourself looking in the mirror. Do you see the beauty in who you are, or do you focus on imperfections? How do you see yourself when you look at your reflection?

▶ SPIRIT STONES

Spirit stones are stones that have been drawn or written on with positive symbols or words, or designs that feel calming to you. They are stones that can be used as a self-care intervention—e.g. creating them for a relaxation activity, using them as worry stones, keeping one in your pocket or someplace nearby as a reminder of encouragement, healing, support, etc., giving them as gifts to others, putting one on a healing shelf, adding one to a Self-Care Kit, or leaving them for others as a random act of kindness.

MATERIALS

Flat and round beach stones (these can be gathered outside or bought at a craft or garden store)

One or more of the following: acrylic ink pens for crafting, permanent ink pens, permanent chalk paint pens

DIRECTIONS

- Prepare the stones by washing them in warm water, and allow them to dry thoroughly.

- Think of words or simple pictures and symbols you'd like to draw on the stones. Here are some words to get you started: DREAM, CALM, HEAL, PLAY, LAUGH, PERSEVERE, RELAX, INSPIRE, BELIEVE, BREATHE, EXPLORE, SPARKLE, PEACE, LOVE, HOPE, JOY, IMAGINE, MAGIC, SHINE, COURAGE. Here are simple pictures and symbols to get you started: peace sign, rainbow, heart, flower, smiley face, sun, star, moon, rune symbols.

- Draw or write on your stones—make sure to follow instructions that accompany the pens you are using.

- Allow the stones to dry.

Release what doesn't help you

It is challenging to let go of events in the past that have caused hurt feelings or harm. On the one hand, it's important to learn what you can from these experiences—for example, to remember and honor anything that came out of that experience that shaped any part of you today. But it's also healthy to let go of the parts of it that are sticking around without a purpose. One thing that may help you let go of something from the past is to have a ritual to help you release it. By writing down the things you want to let go of, you start the process of intention in letting it go. I've included some activities that are favorites among the teens I work with.

▶ TEA WISHES

Tea Wishes are tiny messages written on emptied tea bags and then lit. The Wishes rise into the air and then turn to ash. It's rather fun! However, since this activity involves matches and burning paper, a word of caution is required. Make sure you've asked permission to do this activity and/or have adult supervision. Also, make sure you choose an area where there are no materials that would burn easily if by chance your tea bag veers off while still in flames. Blacktop, pavement, sand, and dirt driveways are good examples of spaces that work well for this activity. A windless day works best as well. Be safe and use common sense, since fires can start quickly.

MATERIALS

> 1 or more tea bags
>
> Non-flammable plate
>
> Pencil or pen
>
> Matches or lighter
>
> An outdoor space cleared of any debris

DIRECTIONS

- Trim off the top of a tea bag. If your tea bag has a staple in it, cut below the staple.

- Empty all of the tea leaves from the tea bag.

- Trim the bottom of the tea bag. Both ends need to be trimmed and open.

- Think of something you wish to release or let go, and write it down on the tea bag.

- Form the tea bag into a cylinder and place it upright on a plate.

- Light the top of the tea bag.

- The tea bag will burn down to the bottom and then lift into the air.

- Repeat as needed.

▶ ELEPHANT PICTURE

Elephants are extraordinary animals known for many characteristics—their large size, their caring nature, and their memory—to name a few.

In this activity the elephant represents a strong nurturing animal that is going to honor the pain you have experienced in life, and it is going to carry that pain so you no longer need to. This is metaphorically speaking, of course, but it provides a medium for naming those experiences and providing a practice in guided imagery. You can use the drawing on the "Elephant" worksheet.

MATERIALS

Drawing of an elephant (you can draw your own if you like)

Newsprint paper

Pencil or pen

Scissors

Decoupage glue

Acrylic paint, watercolors, coloring pencils, and/or markers

Paint brush

DIRECTIONS

- Using the newsprint paper, write down any experiences you wish you could let go, forget, or release. Consider the experiences that burden you or resurface from time to time. You can name and describe these experiences in as little or as much detail as feels right to you.

- Cut what you wrote into small sections or thin strips.

- Working with one section of paper at a time, use a paint brush to apply a thin coat of decoupage glue to one side. If you want no one to see any of the words you've written, make sure to apply the glue to the side of paper that you wrote on.

- Place that piece of paper onto the elephant, keeping it inside the drawing. Decoupage glue makes paper more pliable, so if part of the paper extends outside of the elephant, use your paint brush to push it back within the lines. Apply gentle pressure as needed, making sure the paper adheres to the picture. It's okay if the paper is a bit bumpy and uneven, as it will give your picture textural detail.

- Repeat as needed, until all of your paper strips and sections are used.

- If there are blank areas remaining in the elephant, you can repeat the former step using plain strips of newsprint.

- Allow the picture to dry.

- Color or paint your elephant if desired and/or add embellishments such as sequins, string, or glitter.

- Allow the elephant to dry.

Elephant

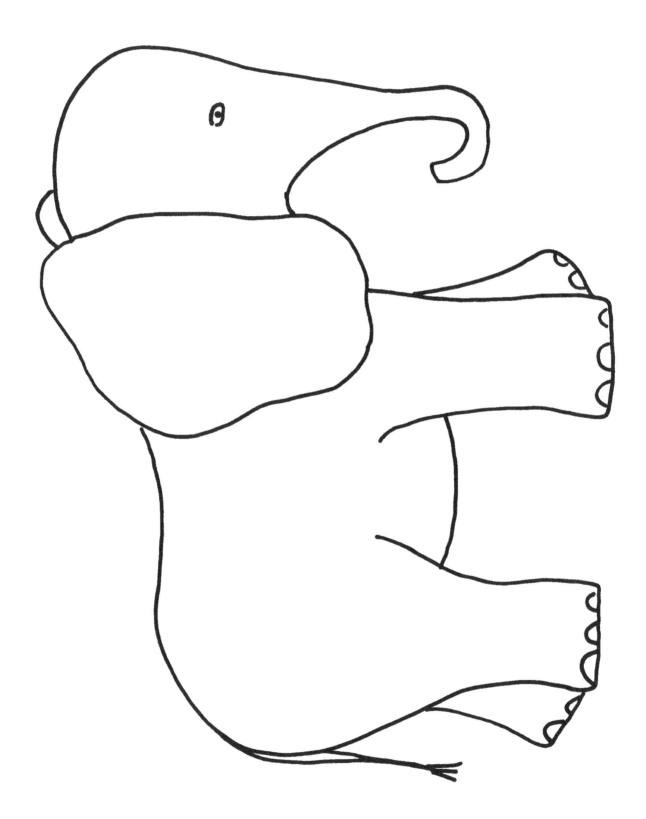

How to use your elephant picture as a practice in guided imagery:

- When experiences from the past or present are sitting heavy on your mind and heart, picture the elephant holding onto them for you. Imagine this elephant as a caring entity that hears and feels your pain, and wants to help you heal. Envision the elephant taking the hurt from you, holding on to it, and carrying it for you instead. This guided imagery practice can be used anytime you feel the need to be heard, seen, honored, and nurtured.

▶ DISSOLVING PAPER

There is a unique version of paper that dissolves in water called "water soluble paper" or "dissolving paper." It usually has to be special ordered, unless you are lucky enough to have a local stationary shop that sells it. You can write and draw on dissolving paper just like you would with regular paper. However, like its name suggests, dissolving paper actually dissolves in water. For this reason, it's an exceptional art medium for this activity in which you release something that no longer helps you.

MATERIALS

Dissolving paper

Colored pencils

Bowl or large jar

Water

Spoon, dowel, or stick for stirring

DIRECTIONS

- Make sure your work area is very dry.

- Write or draw anything you wish to release or let go of onto a piece of the dissolving paper. The youth I work with choose things such as unwanted habits, adverse life experiences, repetitive thoughts or compulsions, illness, stressors, intrusive thoughts, family discord, and more.

- Fill a bowl or jar with water but do not fill it to the top. You will need room for the paper (and for stirring).

- Take a moment to reflect on what you've written or drawn.

- Put your paper in the water and stir it—watch it dissolve.

- Visualize letting go of whatever it is you wrote on the paper.

- When you're ready, dispose of the paper-water responsibly— pour it down the sink, flush it down the toilet, or compost it.

Reframe your thoughts

"Reframing" means looking at a thought, a belief, or an experience through a new or different lens. It also means formulating a more realistic or balanced view of something rather than seeing it as all good or all bad. For example, if you frequently say negative things like "My life sucks," "Nothing good ever happens to me," or "I'm ugly," then you could benefit from reframing those thoughts into more positive and/or realistic ones. Changing these negative thoughts into positive thoughts could boost your self esteem and confidence.

Alternatively, there are times when challenging your optimism makes sense as well—for example, if you're in an abusive situation but expect things will improve, or if you have an addiction but don't see a need to quit. In this regard, you could use reframing to challenge your own optimism in these situations.

Reframing is simply a tool to keep yourself in check—to help you monitor if you're getting stuck in one perspective or another, and to make sure you're allowing yourself to see the bigger picture of what's going on. The following activities will help you practice reframing.

▶ LIGHT VS DARK—A PHOTOGRAPHIC STORY ·····················

In this activity you will be photographing two different representations of the same location—one representation will focus on the negative aspects of the location, and the other will focus on the positive.

MATERIALS

Camera—a phone camera works well for this activity, as does a regular camera

DIRECTIONS

- Find a location you want to photograph. It could be a park, a trail, a library, a building, your home, etc.

- Go through the location and photograph as many details as you can to show the beauty and positive aspects of this location. Examples of what you might photograph include:

  — Beautiful and inviting objects found in this space. If you are inside this might include an architectural detail (e.g. the way a stair banner curls at the bottom of the rail), the binding on a book, a treasured item on a shelf, or a comfortable place to rest. If you are outside you can photograph natural items such as acorns, grass, flowering plants, leaves, or shells; architectural details on nearby buildings; blue sky and/or clouds; or a place you'd feel comfortable sitting for a moment.

  — Any bright spaces where light or sunlight is shining.

  — Appealing patterns and colors. If you are inside you might find these on wallpaper, floorboards, tiles, furniture fabric, or wall art. If you are outside you might find these on brick or stone structures, leaf patterns, flowers, rocks, stairwells, urban art, snowflakes and ice, or tree roots and bark.

  — If people are in this space, capture any smiles or tender moments such as people holding hands, someone feeding the birds, a pet sleeping soundly, etc.

- Next, go through the same space and focus on all the dark and less attractive features of the space.

- Photograph the dark spaces and shadows.

- Take pictures of any litter, graffiti, or debris if you're at an outside location.

- If you're inside a home there may be piles of laundry, a sink full of dirty dishes, an unclean bathtub or sink, or an unmade bed.

- Look for anything dusty, rusty, broken, or in a state of decay.

- If there are people around, photograph those who look upset or uncomfortable.

- Take photos of objects that indicate something unsettling or troubling could be happening here.

- Now that you have a collection of photos, create a photo collage from each perspective—one collage of the "positive side" and one collage of the "negative side." If you are using a regular camera, print out your favorite photos from each series and arrange them in a collage. If you are using digital photos, you can arrange them in a collage using a photo collage app.

- Look over your photos and reflect on how you were able to choose two differing lenses for the same location. You were able to tell two very different stories about the same place just by switching your lens and changing the way you look at something.

This activity illuminates how we have the ability to reflect on our surroundings in various ways. We can choose to focus on the positive or focus on the negative. We can even choose to see both perspectives simultaneously. This ability to "reframe" how we view the world is the same ability that allows us to change how we think, behave, or act. The next time you find yourself thinking a situation or experience to be all negative, use your reframing skills to think of any positive aspects that may also be present.

▶ THAT WHICH GREW FROM THE DARK

For the purpose of this activity, "dark experiences" include those in which your safety or worldview was compromised, your voice silenced, your heart broken, and/or you landed in the midst of a seemingly insurmountable challenge. When you experience something like this it may be difficult to consider that anything positive could grow out it. When possible, however, it's empowering to turn that dark experience around and to look for something positive that resulted from it. The ability to embrace something positive from such an experience takes time—often weeks, months, or even years after the event. In counseling we refer to this as "posttraumatic growth."

Posttraumatic growth tends to occur in five general areas. Sometimes people who must face major life crises develop a sense that new opportunities have emerged from the struggle, opening up possibilities that were not present before. A second area is a change in relationships with others. Some people experience closer relationships with some specific people, and they can also experience an increased sense of connection to others who suffer. A third area of possible change is an increased sense of one's own strength—"if I lived through that, I can face anything." A fourth aspect of posttraumatic growth experienced by some people is a greater appreciation for life in general. The fifth area involves the spiritual or religious domain. Some people experience a deepening of their spiritual lives; however, this deepening can also involve a significant change in one's belief system (Post Traumatic Growth Research Group n.d.).

"That which Grew from the Dark" explores these positive aspects from a negative, or even life-changing, experience.

MATERIALS

Paper

Drawing supplies such as pens, markers, and/or pencils

DIRECTIONS

- Think about a time in your life when you had a dark experience such as a loss, a traumatic event, or life-changing moment.

- Draw a line across the middle of your paper. This line will represent the ground—below the line is earth, and above the line is air.

- Below the center line (in the ground), draw something to represent this "dark" experience—it can be a scribble, a black circle, a broken heart, or other symbol of your choosing (e.g. a dark seed). You can also write about the experience or label it instead of drawing. If you choose to write, make sure it's written in the ground below the center line.

- Look over the image or words you added. Reflect on how this experience has changed you and the way you live your life now because of it.

- Next, draw a line that extends vertically from the item you drew or from the words you wrote. Draw that line to the surface of the ground.

- Draw a flower stem or a tree trunk growing from line. If you can think of one positive outcome from your dark experience, draw a singular flower or tree canopy from the line you drew. If you can think of more positive outcomes, create tree branches extending from the tree trunk, or shoots extending from the flower stem.

- Label each flower or tree branch/canopy with a positive outcome that resulted from your dark experience. For example, "I became a more compassionate person," or "I met a community of supportive people I now call friends."

- You have now illustrated your own version of "That Which Grew from the Dark." Feel free to add to this picture as you develop or discover new areas of growth.

▶ BLACKED OUT WORDS

A trending activity in expressive arts is blacking out words on a page (e.g. from a magazine or book) so that only certain words remain. The remaining words typically create a new sentence, idea, or thought. Sometimes all but one word is blacked out—that one word is typically a stand-alone message in and of itself, such as "Be" or "Love."

To practice your reframing skills, Blacked Out Words is an activity where you use the same piece of writing to create two distinctly different messages—a negative message and then a positive one.

MATERIALS

Black marker (permanent ones work best)

Pencil

"Blacked Out Words" worksheet

Photocopier (you will need two copies of the handout)

DIRECTIONS

- Read through the "Blacked Out Words" worksheet to familiarize yourself with the content.

- Label one copy of your worksheet "negative" and the other copy "positive."

- Start with the negative one first:

  — Look over the worksheet—notice any words that strike you as negative, sad, depressing, or foreboding. Lightly underline those words in pencil.

  — Note any basic structure words (e.g. I, and, but, the) that come before the words you chose. Are you able to create a negative or pessimistic statement by putting any of those structure words with the underlined words in sequential order? This step takes some trial and error as well as patience, so take your time with it.

  — If the above step is too challenging, you can choose one word from the worksheet that feels negative to you.

  — Once you've decided on the word or words you will use, black out all the other words so that only your chosen word/s remain.

- Next, go to your worksheet labeled "positive."

  — Look over the worksheet and notice any words that strike you as positive, uplifting, encouraging, or happy. Lightly underline those words in pencil.

— Note any basic structure words (e.g. I, and, but, the) that come before the words you chose.

— Are you able to create a positive message by putting any of the structure words with the underlined words in sequential order?

— Again, you can choose one word from the worksheet that feels positive to you.

— Once you've decided on the word or words you will use, black out all the other words so that only your chosen word/s remain.

• Now compare the two different worksheets. One has a negative message and the other has a positive message, yet both are created from the same content.

The way you take in information about the world depends heavily on your viewpoint. If you have a negative view, you're going to notice more of the bad things in a situation. If you have a positive view, you're going to see more of the good. The next time you find yourself thinking or feeling negatively about a situation, try thinking about it through a different lens.

*

Blacked Out Words

· ·

In this life you will have choices. In this world, you CAN make a difference. There is good in this world, but there will be times when you have to look for it. There will even be times when you have to *be* it. I cannot promise that you will be happy all the time, or that you will see the beauty in each and every moment, or that you will feel joy more times than not. Sometimes you will hurt. Sometimes you will feel pain—this is part of being alive and human. Sometimes you will find yourself in a dark place. When this happens, do not succumb to the lure of giving up. Do not give in to isolation and despair.

I know it can feel impossible, but reach deep inside and find your inner light. Keep it burning. Keep it alive. Will it to shine. Do not get lost in the darkness. Embrace your power—your beautiful unique self—and rise up against the dark. Be seen. Be heard. Live.

Examples of contrasting messages

You can be happy/You can feel joy	You can feel despair
You can find your inner light	You can get lost in the darkness
Life can be beauty	Life can be pain
I will rise up	I will give up
I will be heard/I will be seen	I cannot be heard/I cannot be seen
Look for the beauty in each and every moment	Look at the pain of being alive
I rise	I succumb
I feel joy	I feel pain/I feel hurt

▶ REFRAMING A THOUGHT: ALL OR NOTHING THINKING

All or Nothing Thinking includes the thoughts we have with words in them like "always," "never," and "every time":

"I *always* mess things up."

"*Every time* my teacher calls on me I say something stupid."

"I'm *never* going to get this done."

The problem with All or Nothing Thinking is it's very limiting—it can make a person feel like there's no possibility for change. You can modify your thoughts, however, into ones that allow for the possibility of a different outcome.

- Choose an All or Nothing thought you have had recently and write it here:

  _____

- What new thought can you replace the All or Nothing statement above with? For example, instead of thinking, "I always mess things up," I will replace that thought with, "Mistakes happen."

  _____

  _____

Focus on what you have control of

In any situation you will find there are things that are within your control—and things that are not. If you focus on things that are not in your control, you will likely create more stress for yourself. But if you focus on the things you do have control over, you can act on those things for positive change. For example, what if a "friend" says something mean and untrue about you on a social media site?

What's not in your control:

- your friend's behavior

- how other people respond to your friend's comment or post

- social media in general.

What's in your control:

- You can ask your friend to remove it, as well as ask the friend to make a statement on the same social media site that the information was in error.

- If your friends are not doing things that make them caring and respectful friends, you can choose not to be friends with them.

- You can block the friend from your online accounts.

- Ask a trusted adult for help.

- Make new, healthier friends. If you end up making new friends from a different school or out of town, you can connect with those friends during after-school hours for added support and encouragement.

- Join after-school activities (e.g. clubs, sports, classes, etc.) to meet and make new friends.

- Set the example of what you want a friend to be like.

- Set the example of how you want others to treat each other online.

- Use your calming strategies for managing the moments when you feel upset.

- "Hold your head high"—use a confident posture when you're around others who want to see you fail. Even if you feel small and defeated, a confident posture will show others and yourself that can stand tall in the midst of negativity.

- Be respectful and kind to yourself and others.

You can use the "What's in Your Control?" worksheet to brainstorm a dilemma of your own if needed.

What's in Your Control?

• •

1. Give the situation a title:

2. Describe the situation:

_____

_____

3. Complete this table.

What is *not* in your control in this situation?	What is in your control in this situation?

Ask for help

An important self-care skill is knowing when to ask for help. Some people find asking for help easy where others may find it extremely difficult. There are many reasons people do not ask for help when they need it, from cultural reasons to situational ones. However, there are moments when you will need or want help in your lifetime, whether it's day-to-day help (e.g. "I need help with this math problem") or help with bigger problems (e.g. "something awful happened and I don't know what to do about it").

One way to get better at asking for help is to practice. Practice gives you experience, and experience gives you familiarity. The more familiar you become with asking for help, the more automatic it becomes. If it's difficult for you to ask for help, you can practice by asking for help with small things, for example, "I need help reaching that glass. Could you reach it for me?" If someone declines to help you, ask someone else, or try it again yourself. The more you practice asking for help, the easier it should become.

Also, remind yourself as often as needed that we all need help and assistance sometimes, even you—this is simply part of being human. It's okay to ask for help, and you are certainly worthy of any support that comes your way.

Scales

When I meet with tweens and teens we frequently create scales for various feelings and symptoms including anger, difficulty focusing, anxiety, and depression. I use scales that are numbered from 1–5. A "1" on these scales mean you are feeling most like yourself and are not experiencing symptoms. A "5" represents feeling your worst. Scales are a valuable tool in self care for the following reasons:

- They provide a language for what you're experiencing. It's much easier to talk about your symptoms and feelings when there is a number to speak of, rather than needing to describe everything in detail. For example, "I was at a 2 this morning, but now I'm at a 4" is much easier to say than, "This morning I was feeling okay. I might have started to feel a little anxious but maybe I wasn't noticing my symptoms as much. By afternoon I started to feel a little uncomfortable and noticed my heart was beating faster, my mouth was dry, and my stomach started to hurt. Now I'm worried about having a panic attack." Scales can help you simplify what you need and want to say, which is especially helpful when you're too upset or anxious to think or communicate clearly.

- Once you've completed a scale it becomes much easier to recognize when you're moving into a higher or lower level of functioning because you've already done the work to recognize the difference between each level of symptoms.

- Scales provide tangible numbers that are helpful when you want to set a goal. Here are some examples: "I want to manage my anger at a level 2 at least half of the time;" "I'm feeling at a 4 right now and I want get back down to a 2 or 1;" "When I go to my mother's house later I want to keep my anger at a 3 or lower."

- Once you know what you experience at each level of the scale, you can write down what helps at each level.

- A completed scale is an informative resource for yourself, your loved ones, and care providers—it's a tool that reminds yourself and others to know how to support you during challenging moments.

I have included Scales worksheets for Anger, Anxiety, and Depression. There is also a blank scale for a feeling or symptom not covered here.

My Anger Scale

When my anger is at a…	I feel…(cross out anything you don't feel)	I also feel…	And this is what helps me at this level…
Level 1	Calm and relaxed.		
Level 2	A little bothered or impatient but in control.		
Level 3	Annoyed and irritable. My heart rate has increased a little; my face feels warm.		
Level 4	Angry and upset. My face is red; I'm yelling or raising my voice; I'm arguing/not listening; I'm threatening others or saying things that are not respectful.		
Level 5	Explosive and raging. I'm harming myself, others, or property. I might black out and not remember what I've done when I get this angry.		

*

My Anxiety Scale

When my anxiety is at a...	I feel...(cross out anything you don't agree with or feel)	I also feel...	And this is what helps me at this level...
Level 1	Calm—nothing is worrying me. I feel comfortable, carefree, and relaxed.		
Level 2	I feel alert, maybe a little tense. I may be starting to feel a little anxious or uncomfortable, but it's not getting in the way of what I need or want to do.		
Level 3	I feel mildly anxious, worried, and/or uncomfortable.		
Level 4	Moderately anxious. I have a headache and/or stomach ache; my mouth feels dry; I'm scared I'm going to have an anxiety attack.		
Level 5	Panicked—I'm having an anxiety attack. I feel dizzy/lightheaded; my heart is racing.		

My Depression Scale

When my depression is at a…	I feel…(cross out anything you do not feel or agree with)	I also feel…	And this is what helps me at this level…
Level 1	Fine—or even great! I don't have any depressive symptoms at this level.		
Level 2	I'm noticing a slight decrease in my energy and mood. However, I'm getting all my responsibilities done and I'm not falling behind in school or relationships.		
Level 3	Concerned—I'm starting to feel exhausted and overwhelmed. I've started to fall behind in responsibilities. I just want to sleep all day.		
Level 4	Depressed, exhausted, and overwhelmed. I feel like giving up. I feel like no one cares about me.		
Level 5	Unsafe and/or suicidal. I need immediate help. I need to call 911, call crisis support, or go to the emergency room/hospital.		

My Scale

When my _____ is at a...	I feel...	And this is what helps me at this level...
Level 1		
Level 2		
Level 3		
Level 4		
Level 5		

Use reminders for self-care and coping skills

The following activities help you take care of yourself by being prepared ahead of time to do so.

If you've tried or used any of the self-care and coping skills noted in this book, then you'll have a solid foundation for creating reminders for self-care and coping skills in this section.

▶ SELF-CARE PLANNING FOR MICRO MOMENTS

This activity helps you organize your self-care strategies into specific time frames so you know which ones to use when you have a certain amount of time. If you have only 30 seconds to spare, for example, your self-care options will be different than if you have 30 minutes. By devising a plan for these "micro moments" you become better prepared to carry out the self care you need.

MATERIALS

Piece of paper (standard size)

Pencil or pen

Optional: "Self-Care Planning Template" worksheet

DIRECTIONS

You can use the "Self-Care Planning Template" worksheet or make your own.

- To make your own, fold a piece of paper into six different sections by doing the following:

  — Fold the paper into thirds.

  — Unfold the paper.

  — Now fold the paper in half in the opposite direction in which you originally folded it.

- Label each section as follows: 30 seconds; 5 minutes or less; 5–15 minutes; 15 minutes–1 hour; 1 hour; 3 hours or more.

- Fill in each section with self-care strategies you can use to fit within each time frame. Here are some examples of what might go in each time category:

30 seconds

- Take a deep cleansing breath.

- Shake all the stress from your body.

- Stretch your arms into the sky.

- Give yourself an affirmation or positive message.

- Think of something you're grateful for.

- Drink some water.

5 minutes or less

- Drink a full glass of water.

- Take three deep, cleansing breaths.

- Do some quick, simple stretches.

- Listen to a favorite song.

- Send a friend a positive message.

- Open a window and breathe some fresh air.

5–15 minutes

- Make a "to-do" list for the day.

- Write in a journal.

- Sit in a sunbeam and let the sun warm your face and skin.

- Listen to music you need for the moment (e.g. relaxing, motivating, etc.).

- Make a phone call to schedule a needed appointment.

15 minutes–1 hour

- Take a hot shower or a bubble bath.

- Paint your nails.

- Soak your feet.

- Meditate.

- Do some stretches.

- Make a pitcher of iced herbal tea.

- Make a pitcher of infused water.

- Go for a brisk walk.

- Make and drink a nutritious smoothie.

1 hour

- Go for a walk.

- Call a good friend and catch up.

- Bake something healthy for tomorrow's breakfast, e.g. whole grain muffins.

- Read a book or listen to an audio book or podcast about a self-care topic.

- Do a bentonite clay face mask.

- Soak in a bathtub with Epsom salts.

3 hours or more

- Go to a class (e.g. yoga, meditation, sound healing).

- Go to an appointment (e.g. counseling, massage, hair).

- Meet up with a friend.

- Explore a local trail.

- Create some artwork.

- Make healthy snacks or meals for the upcoming week.

- Go on a day trip—explore a new place nearby.

- Put together a Self-Care Kit (see Self-Care Kit handout).

Photocopy this list and keep a copy in your backpack, purse, or locker. Whenever you discover a new self-care option, add it to your list. Next time you find yourself with a few spare moments or in need of self care, you will have a quick reference guide for what you can do to improve your wellbeing.

*

Self-Care Planning Template

List the self-care activities you can do within each time frame.

30 seconds	5 minutes or less	5–15 minutes

15 minutes–1 hour	1 hour	3 hours or more

▶ SELF-CARE CARDS

Self-Care Cards are a deck of cards you make where each card contains one of the following:

- a quote/word that inspires or motivates you

- an image and/or word of something that makes you feel calm

- an image and/or word that makes you smile or laugh

- something positive others have said about you

- a self-care intervention

- something you're proud of

- a calming strategy to use.

One card, for example, might feature a picture of kittens or puppies because it makes you smile; another card might have instructions for a yoga pose that reduces anxiety. You can make as many cards as you need and they can be as simple or elaborate as you want based on the materials you have and/or your creativity. I've seen many decks created from manila folders where only words were added to the cards—these work just as beautifully as the ones made with multiple images and artistic embellishment.

MATERIALS

"Self-Care Cards" worksheet

Blank card stock or thin cardboard (manila folders and recycled cereal boxes work well for these)

Decoupage glue and/or white glue

Markers and/or ink pens

White paper

Patterned papers (optional)

Calming images (these can be drawn, cut from magazines, or printed)

Paint brush

Scissors

DIRECTIONS

- Use the "Self-Care Cards" worksheet to organize your card ideas. This will help you plan what you need for materials and resources.

- Cut your card stock or thin cardboard into card shapes and size—you can choose how big or small you want the cards, and you can also choose the shape. The number of cards will depend on the number of ideas you want to include in your deck.

- If you're using recycled cardboard for your cards, you may want to glue plain or patterned paper on the sides that have printed product material. This isn't necessary, but it adds a cleaner look to your card deck.

- Design one card at a time. If you have limited materials to work with, you can create each card using written words only. For example, if watching a sunset is calming to you and you want it in your deck, you can simply write, "watching a sunset."

- If you've used any glue on your cards, allow the glue to dry thoroughly before stacking your cards together in a deck.

Self-Care Cards are a valuable resource to have on hand, especially if you're the kind of person who has trouble remembering how to care for your wellbeing when you are feeling stressed out. When you feel upset or off-balance, look through your card deck to remind yourself of ways to relax and care for your body and mind.

Self-Care Cards

· ·

Quotes and words that inspire me:

_____

_____

_____

Images of things or words that make me feel calm or happy:

_____

_____

_____

Images of things or words that make me smile and laugh:

_____

_____

_____

Positive things others have said about me:

_____

_____

_____

Self-care activities I can do:

_____

_____

_____

*

Calming strategies I can use:

_____

_____

_____

Things I've accomplished and/or am proud of:

_____

_____

_____

Other things I want to add to my self-care cards:

_____

_____

_____

▶ SELF-CARE KITS

Self-Care Kits are a collection of items that you put together ahead of time for moments when you need a boost of self care. They are meant to be small and portable so you can toss them in a backpack, purse, glove compartment, or other small space. Think of them as mini first aid kits for self care.

MATERIALS

Container for your Self-Care Kit—e.g. a makeup bag; a small, recycled box; a recycled container from a box of matches; or a lozenge tin

SELF-CARE KIT FOR WHEN YOU'RE UPSET, E.G. GOING THROUGH A BREAK-UP OR GRIEVING

Eye drops

Small pack of tissues

Makeup/cosmetics

Throat lozenges (if your throat gets tight from crying)

SELF-CARE KIT FOR ANXIETY

Homeopathic or herbal relaxation drops/lozenges

A reminder to breathe

Worry stone or crystal

Something to fidget with

Picture of something that makes you smile (e.g. your pet or best friend)

SELF-CARE KIT FOR ILLNESS/NOT FEELING WELL

Tissues

Cough drops

Medicine or remedies

Medicinal tea bag

Aromatherapy oil, e.g. eucalyptus

Lip balm

EVERYDAY CALMING KITS

Inspiring quote or affirmation

Small crystal or good luck charm

Religious or spiritual tokens such as prayer beads and miniature shrine items

Favorite photo

A reminder of a goal you're working toward

List of contact information for friends, family, providers, or crisis services

► CREATE A HEALING SHELF

A Healing Shelf is a space set aside for objects that feel healing to you. It can be a space other than a shelf, such as the top of a bureau, a locker, or a nook in a bookcase. Your choice of items will be unique to you and your needs, but here are items to consider:

Candle

Framed picture or collage of people who care about you and support you

Framed quote or mantra

Trinkets from loved ones to remind yourself you are loved and supported

Crystals and gems that feel healing to you

Cards from self-help decks, e.g. an angel card or animal totem card

Aromatherapy oils

Items from nature you've found (e.g. feathers, heart-shaped stones)

Artwork that feels healing

Sage spray

A journal

Healing Shelves create spaces of serenity and reflection that can be calming and nurturing to look upon or to use the items. Change your items around as needed to reflect your current needs.

► MAKE A SELF-CARE "SPELL BOOK"

I make these "Spell Books" with youth who are fans of wizardry stories and/or love the creative challenges involved in this project. Self-Care "Spell Books" look spooky and archaic, and contain "recipes and spells" for self care. You can use the "Spell Book Template" worksheet.

TOXIC PEOPLE AND SITUATIONS TO STAY AWAY FROM:

Herbal Teas:
list your favorite teas

What will you try to improve your sleep?

Earthing
sit against a tree,
or sit upon a rock,
or lay down in the grass,
or in bare feet you may walk.

MATERIALS

A hardcover sketchbook is recommended, but I've also made simple sketchbooks by folding plain paper in half and stapling a cardstock cover in place

Alphabet foam letters or raised alphabet letters/stickers that spell "SPELL BOOK" or "SPELLS"

Pencil

Hot glue gun and hot glue sticks

Paper towels

Decoupage glue

Paint brushes for glue and paints

Acrylic paints: black, white, gold

Optional: "Spell Book Template"

DIRECTIONS

- Attach or glue your letters to the cover of your book to spell "SPELL BOOK" or "SPELLS."

- Lightly draw a spider web onto your cover using pencil.

- Heat up your glue gun. Carefully apply hot glue along the lines you drew for the spider web. Allow the glue to dry.

- If you want to add any other raised details on your cover, do so with the hot glue— e.g. you can make dots along the edges of the cover, a spider, or a lightening bolt.

- When done with the glue gun, make sure to unplug it and set it aside safely.

- Tear a few paper towels into strips.

- Use a paint brush to apply decoupage glue in and around your letters and other raised areas.

- Apply a layer of paper towel over the letters, the spider web, and any raised areas.

- Use your paint brush to push the paper towel in and around these raised areas. If needed, apply additional pieces of paper towel and/or apply more glue. You will likely need to be persistent and push the paper towel into place a few times. You want the paper towel to adhere as much as possible to your raised areas so you can see the details as clearly as possible.

- Once your raised areas have been decoupaged with a layer of paper towel, do the same for the flat areas of your cover.

- Allow the paper towel layer/s to dry thoroughly.

- Optional—If needed, add another layer of paper towel in areas that need fixing. Allow any additional layers of paper towel to dry.

- Apply a thin coat of black paint over your entire cover. You will need to lightly push your paint brush into the crevices between your letters and raised areas in order for paint to get into these tight spaces.

- Optional—While the black paint is still wet you can add a small amount of white paint to make a grayish tone to your cover. Dab a small amount of white paint on your paint brush and paint over the black. This will create inconsistent shades of black and white giving an antiquated look to your cover.

- Apply a very small amount of gold paint to your fingertips and rub your fingertips together. Use your fingertips to rub the gold paint over the raised areas of your cover.

- Allow your book to dry.

- If desired, use the "Spell Book Template" worksheet to add pre-designed "spells" and recipes to your book. Color them if you like, then cut and glue them into your pages.

- Add your own "spells" and recipes too—these can include herbal recipes for tea, tinctures, and balms for self care; yoga poses and hand mudras; affirmations and mantras; and lists of self-care strategies to use.

HOCUS FOCUS SPRAY:

Add 2 tsp. isopropyl alcohol to a 2 oz. spray bottle.

Add 5 drops of peppermint essential oil AND 10 drops of rosemary essential oil.

Fill remainder of bottle with filtered or distilled water.

Shake gently, then spray. (spray it in the air around you)

Confidence Spell:

breathe in while you think to yourself: "breathe in strength" then breathe out while you think to yourself: "breathe out fear."

Repeat as needed.

Calming Trick:

Lay on a floor or bed and put your legs up against the wall.

Lie in this position for 10-15 minutes.

HYDRATION POTION:

Place slices from half a cucumber in a large pitcher or jar. Cover with water till container is 2/3 full. Let chill for 2 hours.

Pour over ice and drink.

▶ SELF CARE DURING ADJUSTMENT AND LIFE-ALTERING CHANGES

Change comes in many forms. There are small changes in life like adjusting to glasses for the first time or getting a new pet. But there are changes—life-altering changes—that require a whole different set of resources (internal and external) to manage. Life-altering changes include the death of a loved one, leaving home or a long-term relationship for the first time, transitioning to a new identity, "coming out," bringing a new child or sibling into the family, a traumatic event, etc.

As you know already, change is messy and exhausting—sometimes even the "happy" changes can be messy and exhausting too. Change requires patience even when each and every cell in your body is screaming that it wants things to feel comfortable and okay and familiar RIGHT NOW.

In an ideal world, at least in my ideal world, each of us would be compassionate and open-minded to other people's experiences, especially during these life-changing ones. In addition, we would also be gentler with ourselves.

The following are reminders and tips for getting through those life-altering changes, as well as how to help others going through the same:

- Reach out to friends, loved ones, and professionals who can offer support.

- Get plenty of rest, nutrients, fresh air, and hydration.

- Find an outlet for your emotions—e.g. art, music, counseling, exercise, journaling.

- Allow yourself the space to cry if needed.

- Keep a mini Self-Care Kit with you.

- Find "your people"—join an online or local support group of others going through the same or similar experience as you.

- Remind yourself that change is uncomfortable and it's okay to feel that discomfort.

- Keep a Gratitude Journal during this time—I know that sounds counterintuitive, but when you are adjusting to a whole new life, identity, or situation, everything can feel challenging, raw, and unforgivingly bleak. A Gratitude Journal can help bring your mind and awareness to the things that are still going right and still feel familiar. Write down all the positives that happen for you each day, whether it's someone holding the door open for you, watching a new episode of a favorite series, or finding pleasure in a refreshing glass of water.

- Take one photograph a day to document your journey and what you are going through. Even if you never share it with anyone, you can look back and see that yes, this was a difficult change and yes, you survived it. You'll have a solid visual of what you endured.

- Pack yourself some bottled water and a healthy snack for tomorrow.

- Write inspiring quotes and phrases on little notes and leave them where you can find them.

- Watch video clips of things that make you smile.

- As you start to find comfort and routine again, consider finding ways to help others.

- If you feel alone, depressed, or isolated, let your trusted support people know—a best friend, a parent, a doctor or counselor. Be honest. Ask for help.

- If you have thoughts about suicide talk to a trusted adult and/or call your local emergency or crisis support center.

How to be supportive for loved ones facing life-altering changes:

- Tell them, "I'm here if you want to talk."

- If they do talk to you about what's going on, listen. Fight the urge to give advice or judge the people involved…just listen. Let them know, "I'm so glad you talked to me about this."

- Consider dropping off—or mailing—a "care package." Care packages can include items such as:

  — things to soothe red eyes and raw throats from crying—tissues, eye drops, eye masks, ice cream, soup, cough drops or throat lozenges

  — a card that lets them know you are thinking of them

  — natural remedies that help with anxiety, grief, or trauma

  — bubble bath, shower gel, and/or a battery-operated candle (your friend might be stressed enough to leave a candle unattended, so a battery one that flickers like a real candle is a relaxing substitute)

  — a few "nutrient-dense" snacks, e.g. trail mix, dried fruit, nuts, protein bars

  — a special blanket to wrap up in

  — an audio book they'd enjoy

  — a blank journal, an adult coloring book, and some art supplies to get creative

  — a gift card to their favorite coffee place or online store.

- Organize your friends, neighbors, family, and/or colleagues to make and deliver meals to the person and/or their family.

- If your friend or loved one's life-altering change involves their identity, such as being transgender, remind yourself they are still the same person you have always known—use the person's correct pronoun and name (this may take a lot of practice and repeating), and be an ally as much as you possibly can.

- If your friend or loved one's life-altering change involves a death, it's okay to talk about it (unless they ask you not to for now). One of the hardest things for grieving people is when others stop talking about the person or pet that passed away. Many grieving people want to share their memories and stories about their loved one.

- If they have a dog, offer to join them for a walk.

- Spend time with them, especially if they seem to be isolating themselves or "disappearing." Offer to bring a movie and "take-out" (or a snack) to their house.

- Create a daily check in time—e.g. each day at 3 pm check in via text message, phone, or Facebook message to see if they need anything and just to let them know you are there for them.

- Keep the lines of communication open—if you are having difficulty as well, let them know. It's okay to say, "This is a big change for me also, but we will get through it—together."

- Look online for other ways to support your friend through this particular change. Search for key phrases like "how to help my friend going through a breakup."

There are so many more ways to be gentle and real with yourself—and others—during a life-altering change, but I hope these lists serve as a good starting place.

▶ SELF CARE AND SAFETY ON DIFFICULT ANNIVERSARY DATES

Many people who have experienced a traumatic event know that the annual anniversary of that event, and each year thereafter, can be emotionally challenging. There are always exceptions, of course—some people can experience the death of a loved one, a breakup, or a harrowing event and not notice any change in affect or physical symptoms on the anniversary. For many people, however, the anniversary can create a sense of angst and side effects: a feeling of unease, disrupted sleep, a feeling of dread regarding the anniversary, anxiety and restlessness, depression, grief and sadness, lack of focus and decreased attention, irritability, and more.

However, there are ways to care for your mind, body, and spirit prior to the anniversary, and throughout, to get through it (and even feel stronger to deal with it).

- Be proactive. Schedule some self care prior to the anniversary. Examples of self care would be attending a class in yoga, art, or meditation, going to counseling, spending a weekend with friends and loved ones, attending a retreat, getting a massage or going to a spa, getting a one-month gym membership, etc. If you are low on cash or on a tight budget, schedule daily walks with a friend, meditate each day, get creative with art, journaling, or coloring books, have extra bubble baths, eat healthy meals, and/or spend time with loved ones. Whatever it is that relaxes you or feeds your soul, put it in your calendar prior to the anniversary.

- Acknowledge and care for your triggers. For smaller, more manageable triggers, use basic calming skills such as taking deep breaths, taking a brisk walk to burn off excess adrenaline, or calling a supportive friend. In addition, keep Self-Care Kits on hand for when uncomfortable feelings arise. For larger, more intrusive triggers, consider counseling in one of the following "evidence-based practices" that address triggers, phobias, and extreme anxiety:

    — Trauma Focused Cognitive Behavioral Therapy (TFCBT)

    — Eye Movement Desensitization and Reprocessing (EMDR)

    — Prolonged Exposure Therapy (PE)

    — Cognitive Processing Therapy (CPT).

- Acknowledge and commemorate the event in a way that suits your personality and needs. Here is a partial list of ideas:

    — Donate money or donate blood for a cause related to the event.

    — Complete ten acts of kindness (or another chosen number) to "counteract" some of the negative feelings about the anniversary, or complete the acts of kindness in memory of someone who passed away.

    — Create a ritual for yourself where you honor what you have survived and endured—light a special candle for yourself; write down your feelings and thoughts about the event, burn it, and release the ashes; hike up a mountain; say a special prayer.

    — Collect a special item each year near the anniversary. For example, I know a person who buys herself a pair of boots on each anniversary. She loves the quote about walking a mile in someone's shoes—the boots are worn as a reminder of what she has been through and what she can conquer. She wears the boots on days when she needs a little extra "kick." In this way, she honors her trauma anniversary and her own power over the event. I know another person who started collecting angels—she now buys an angel on each year near her trauma anniversary. Yet another person writes a new song each year about what he is still learning from his trauma and how the effects of it weave their way into his life each year. So your "collected item" can be fun and inspirational, it can be in memory of someone, or it can be part of an ongoing story that you tell about your experience with the event.

- Celebrate your survival. Invite friends over and celebrate in a way that makes you feel strong, connected, and proud of what you have survived.

- Quiet reflection. Schedule a section of time where you turn off all screens and distractions. Take that quiet time to reflect on what you have been through and what you have gained as a result.

There are more ways to get through a trauma anniversary—if you need or want more ideas you can research the topic of "trauma anniversaries" online, seek professional support, or reach out to loved ones for additional ideas.

▶ SELF CARE FOR DEPRESSION, GRIEF, AND INERTIA

Each of us has at least one compelling story about our relationship with depression, grief, and inertia (all of which I have nicknamed "The Dark" in this section). For some, The Dark has been a literal entity—e.g. a dark place, or night itself, in which something life-changing or memorable happened. For others The Dark has been a metaphorical presence—an addiction, a mental illness, poverty, a loss, heart break, an impossibly unkind world. The Dark has met each and every one of us, and sometimes it favors one person more than another.

Like Death, The Dark is usually unwelcome, as are the gifts it brings. These gifts are not wrapped in pretty bows—indeed, it is hard to recognize them as gifts at all. But gifts, they are. The bravest people I have ever met have been those who are visited unrelentingly by The Dark, and still wake up each morning. These people have stockpiles of gifts from The Dark—in their homes, their backpacks, their purses, their pockets. They are so overloaded with these gifts there is no more room to put them anywhere. They unwrap these gifts, learn from them, and pass them along, rewrapped in the beautiful ribbons and paper they deserve. They also help others who are visited by The Dark. They hold others' hands, shine a light, say words of comfort. They help each other navigate the unruly world where The Dark lives, and offer maps for escape and evacuation. They are the expert witnesses to The Dark, they know its secrets…and I'm going to share some of those secrets with you.

When The Dark comes to visit…

- Don't stay in bed. When you stay in bed, it's easy for The Dark to get comfortable. You can acknowledge its presence and still set boundaries with it. Do not let it overstay its "welcome." The Dark wants nothing more than to snuggle with you under those warm, heavy blankets. Get out of bed. Take a shower.

- Make yourself a meal and/or something healthy to drink. The Dark can be clever and crude, so you need your A-game today—you will think more clearly with nutrients in your body.

- Make a list of what you need to get done. The Dark is good at sabotaging your efforts to accomplish anything. Circle the priorities. Do at least one of them.

- Check in. Let a loved one know what you are dealing with. The Dark will try to keep you isolated—this makes you more likely to lean in toward The Dark. Lean into a friend instead. Receive kindness; receive love.

- Feel your feelings. Acknowledge all the rawness and discomfort and pain that comes with being in The Dark's presence. Remind yourself you have been here before and survived. Feelings change. Life changes. This is temporary. The Dark will go elsewhere, given time.

- The Dark will offer you a way out. If it tempts you with alcohol, drugs, or self harm in order to silence your feelings, find safer ways to release that emotion and pain. Work out, stomp your feet, scream, shake your fist at The Dark and swear at it, cry your heart out, create a piece of art that expresses the pain you feel, write a song, sing loud, clean your room or your house, vent.

- Be kind to yourself. The Dark can make you tired and vulnerable. Don't let it wear you down so much that you forget to build yourself back up. Find ways to comfort your inner spirit, your inner child, your "now" self. Acknowledge each and every kind thing you do for yourself today and really feel it. Tell yourself positive messages. Remind yourself you are loved, you are needed, you are beautiful.

- Ground yourself. Feel your surroundings. The Dark will try to hide you from the little things that help you feel connected to this life. Take in the feeling of warm socks, cool water, fresh air, soft pillows, warm sunshine, gentle rain…feel all of these things and stay grounded.

- Love. Even if you cannot feel it, act on it. Do something kind for someone else: open the door for them, smile, put a quarter in someone's parking meter, say hello to someone, post a kind or funny message on a friend's social media page, tell someone how much you appreciate them, say thank you, snuggle up with your cat or dog.

- Ask for help. If The Dark has stayed too long, or is visiting too often, talk to a professional about it.

- Acknowledge the gifts that The Dark has given you such as empathy for the suffering that others endure, compassion, generosity, kindness, fortitude, perseverance, courage, creativity, wisdom, gratitude, humility, wit, determination, and more. If you look deeper you may find The Dark has been a rather generous benefactor.

There are more strategies and interventions you can try than what I have covered here. There is medication. There are support groups. There are new studies being published that shed light on The Dark. There are services such as case management and counseling. Do not let The Dark take over the amazingly beautiful human being that you are. There is light in this world and you deserve to feel it.

4

Creative Expression

· ·

Think for a moment about what it takes (or what it would take) for you to share your life story with someone else. Does it take earning that person's trust over a long period of time? Does it require someone who is a good listener? Does it take someone who has experienced something similar?

As important as it is for us to share our experiences and stories with others, there are many reasons people hold back and keep those stories to themselves. There are even those who feel they can't share their stories at all. This happens for many reasons including family secrets, personal secrets, embarrassment, protecting someone else, not feeling they deserve to be heard, having anxiety about sharing, or feeling something bad will happen if they share.

People can feel a sense of relief and validation, however, when they document and share their life experiences, which is why it's imperative to find a way, any way, to tell your story, even if it's just for you or told in a way that honors your need for privacy:

> Every time you tell your story and someone else who cares bears witness to it, you turn off the body's stress responses, flipping off toxic stress hormones like cortisol and epinephrine and flipping on relaxation responses that release healing hormones like oxytocin, dopamine, nitric oxide, and endorphins. Not only does this turn on the body's innate self-repair mechanisms and function as preventative medicine—or treatment if you're sick. It also relaxes your nervous system and helps heal your mind of depression, anxiety, fear, anger, and feelings of disconnection. (Rankin 2012)

There are many ways to share your life story including journaling, blogging, in conversation with friends and loved ones, in a public storytelling forum, or in a private counseling session. There are also creative means for archiving these stories, some of which I've included in this chapter of the book. These particular activities make use of symbols and metaphor which may appeal to those who want a more creative or private way to tell their life story.

▶ AUTOBIOGRAPHICAL LIFE MAPS (ALMS)

An Autobiographical Life Map (ALM) is a map that tells a story about your life. These maps look similar to traditional maps but there is a major difference—instead of symbols representing landmarks, they represent life experiences. For example, a road on a traditional map represents a highway or interstate, but a road on an ALM represents the timeline of someone's life. A mountain range on an ALM represents a series of challenges rather than actual mountains. An area of quicksand on an ALM symbolizes a time you felt you were losing ground.

ALMs are a creative and playful means of telling some or all of your life story. They also provide a non-verbal means for sharing your life story.

Here are some things to consider as you create your ALM:

- You are the one who decides what will be included on your map. You are the creator—you get to choose what gets represented and how it gets represented.

- Your map is not going to look logical and this is to be expected. You might end up with a lighthouse in a swamp or a coral reef next to a desert. These are the intriguing details that make your ALM your own, and tell the story of you.

- If needed you can create your own symbols for your legend, e.g. if you need a symbol for an event not covered on the legend, or if you want to design your own version of a symbol.

- Take your time thinking through the events and matching the symbols for your map—there is a lot to consider and plan. But when the map is done it's gratifying to see your story mapped out in this manner—it's worth the time and effort you put into it.

- The legend is not attached to the map, which means anyone viewing the map will not know what the symbols represent. It's a way to tell your story without giving away all the details or meaning.

MATERIALS

Optional: "Autobiographical Life Map Template" worksheet

"Autobiographical Life Map Legend" worksheet

Paper

Pencil

Colored pencils, markers, and/or watercolor paints

Optional—water and paint brushes (if using watercolor paints)

Newspaper (to place under the map while using markers or paints)

DIRECTIONS

- Think about the key moments and people in your life. Make a list of the ones you want to include on your map.

- Based on your list, consider the age you want to start your map with. Do you start at birth? Do you start at a young age? Or do you start at a more recent time of your life?

- Draw an island to represent your life. You can choose to draw the island as simple or as detailed as you prefer. You can also use the map on the ALM template if that's easier.

- Choose a starting point to make a road. This road will be your timeline, just as if you were creating a timeline of your life. Consider what the first event on your map will be and then decide where to locate a starting point based on that event. You will find a description of various road patterns on the "Autobiographical Life Map Legend" worksheet.

- Each item on the "Autobiographical Life Map Legend" describes an event or experience. Circle the events that match the ones on your list. Number them in order of sequence for when they occurred. If you use a symbol more than once, assign it additional numbers as needed.

- Start penciling in your symbols, putting them in sequential order, adding more roads as needed as you go.

- When you've added all of your events and symbols to the map, look it over. If you need to make any changes then do so.

- Go back and color in your map using color pencils, marker, or watercolors.

- Allow your map to dry.

Autobiographical Life Map

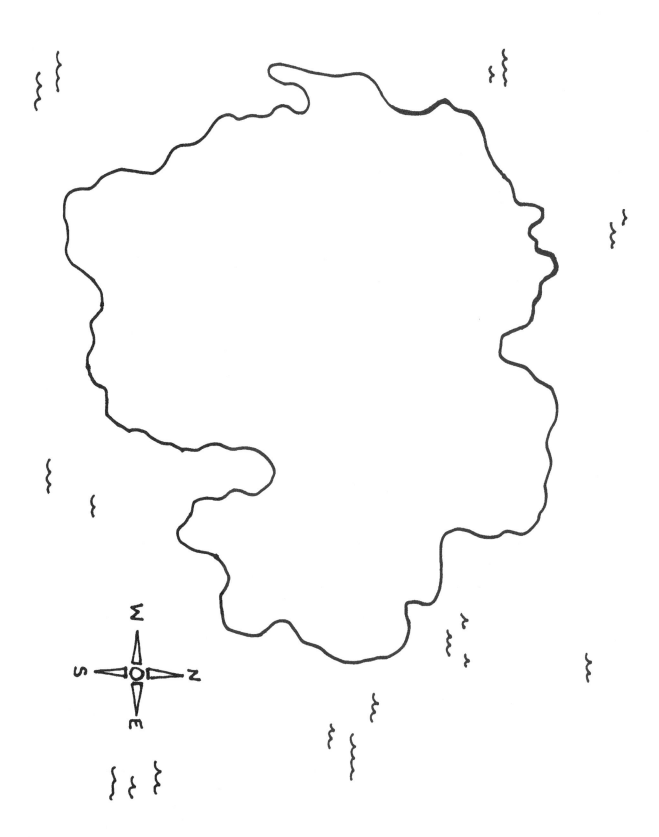

Autobiographical Life Map Legend

Circle the events or symbols you want to include on your Autobiographical Life Map.

A road: Your actual timeline

A dirt road: A period of time in which you felt insecure, unsure, or tried something new

A paved road: A period of time in which you felt confidence

A highway or interstate: A period of time that moved very fast

A rotary or roundabout: A time you felt like things were going in circles or you felt indecisive

A "fork in the road": A time you had to make a major decision

An intersection: A time when you had many choices and options

An ocean: A vast, chaotic time in your life

A lighthouse: A person who tried to help you or lead you to safety

A cliff: A dangerous situation

A sandy beach: A time of respite and relaxation

A rocky shore: A time of getting back on your feet after going through a chaotic situation

A harbor: A time of safety and feeling protected

A forest: Friends and loved ones

Green trees: Healthy, loving friends and family

Autumn trees: Friends/loved ones with whom your relationship has changed

A tree stump: A friend or loved one you cut out of your life

A dead tree: A close friend or loved one who has died

A flower garden: Something you invested a lot of time and energy in (e.g. finishing the school year, training for a race)

*

A lake: Stability in your academic work, relationships, family, or work

A river: A time of success or achievement (the river can intersect your timeline at moments you succeeded or achieved something you had been working for)

A swamp: An area that used to have growth but is now stagnant/no longer growing

Quicksand or a landslide: A time you felt you were losing ground or losing control of something

Mud: A place or time in your life where you felt stuck

A mountain (single): A challenge

A mountain range: Many challenges all at once and/or over a period of time

A volcano: An eruption or awakening of feelings, especially anger

A valley: A time of respite in between more challenging times

A jungle: A time of excessive abundance that came with consequence, e.g. addiction, overspending, or overindulgence

A glacier: A time of repressed feelings, feeling numb, or a fear of expressing feelings

A desert: A time when you desperately wanted more of something in your life, but didn't have the resources to quench that thirst

A cave: A time of self and/or spiritual exploration; going inward; chosen isolation

A town/village: A community that feels supportive

A city: A time or place in your life in which things were going at a faster pace, or there were multiple events happening at once

Unexplored territory: An event or relationship you chose not to engage in

A waterfall: A time of grieving, sadness, tears

A coral reef: A new community of friends or new supports

A circus: A time in your life that felt full of drama

A well: A spiritual, mystical, or religious experience

A windmill: A time of increased energy, creativity, or money

A hospital: A time of deep pain, illness, or injury

Train tracks: A vacation or time of traveling

A tower: A time of isolation; feeling alone

A cemetery: A time when something ended, such as a job, marriage, or relationship

A single gravestone: A loved one's death

A school or library: A time of learning

Jail: A time of paying the consequences for a committing an illegal or harmful act

A bridge (solid): A person or event that helped you reach a goal or achieve success

A bridge (rickety): A person or event that connected you to negative events or people

A playground/park: A time of playfulness, fun, feeling carefree

A treasure chest: A person, animal, object, or event that came into your life at this time that you absolutely treasured

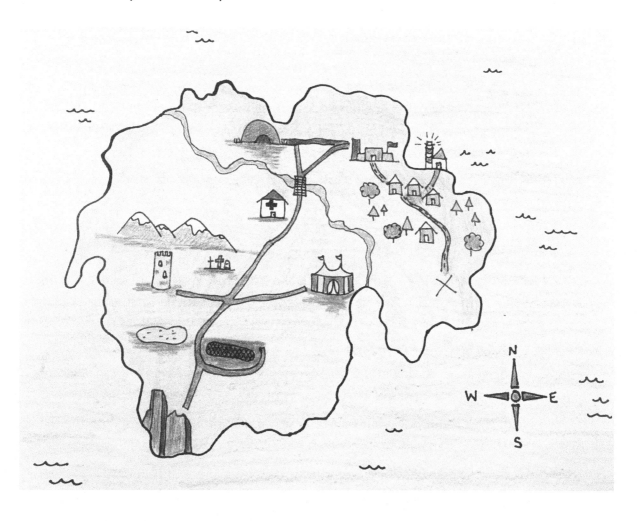

▶ NESTING DOLLS

Nesting Dolls are also known as matryoshkas—they are hollow dolls that nest inside of each other, each doll slightly smaller than the next. They come in a variety of sizes, number, and themes. Although you can buy blank wooden sets to design and create your own, you will design a set on paper for this activity. Try one of the themes listed below for sharing a story about yourself or your life.

MATERIALS

"Nesting Dolls Template" worksheet

Paper

Pencil

Colored pencils or markers

DIRECTIONS

- Choose a theme for your Nesting Dolls set:
  - My timeline: Divide your age by the number of dolls. For example, if you are 15 years old, then each doll represents a span of three years—the smallest doll represents ages 1–3, the next doll represents ages 4–6, and so on till the largest doll represents ages 13–15. Draw life events on each doll that occurred during those years.
  - My personality: Illustrate each doll to represent a different aspect of your personality.
  - My role models: Create each doll to represent a role model that inspires you. Draw or write about the role model on each one.
  - What makes me happy: Decorate the dolls with pictures of things that make your heart feel happy and whole. For example, include your favorite people, animals, foods, events, musicians/bands, art, travel destinations, games, sports, activities, etc.
  - My goals: Each doll in the set represents a goal you have. You can write them directly on the dolls or draw pictures on them to represent each goal.
- Next, think about how you want to design your Nesting Dolls based on the theme you chose.
- Create rough sketches or list your ideas on a blank piece of paper.
- Pencil in your designs on the Nesting Doll Template.
- Color in your designs using pencils and/or marker.

Nesting Dolls Template

▶ AUTOBIOGRAPHICAL FAIRY TALE

People generally think of fairy tales as the "happily ever after" type of stories, but in this activity you'll construct a more traditional fairy tale in which the main character (which will be you) faces a major challenge or life-changing event from your actual life. This can include heartbreak, loss, betrayal, family dysfunction, discrimination, a significant change/adjustment, struggling with identity, or wishing for a different life. Within the story you will choose from a variety of characters and landscapes to represent key people and experiences related to the event.

MATERIALS

Paper and pencil or a computer to write with

"Archetypes and Characters" handout

"Fairy Tale Locations" handout

DIRECTIONS

- Think of a difficult or life-changing experience you've had that you want to write about in your Fairy Tale. If you prefer not to write, consider dictating or illustrating your story instead.

- Next, look at the "Archetypes and Characters" and "Fairy Tale Locations" handouts. Choose the characters you want to represent yourself and the other people involved with the story. Writers of fairy tales often use metaphors and symbolic imagery to emulate the aspects of someone's character or the power of place in a story. Try to do the same. For example, witches are regularly portrayed as mean and vindictive, so if a mean and vindictive person was involved in your life, perhaps a witch is an appropriate character to portray them. Pick one or more settings for your story as well. A tower could be used as a location in the story for a time you felt isolated or excluded/exiled; a beautiful castle could be a location for part of your story in which you felt safe and protected.

- Write and/or illustrate your story as if it were a fairy tale, including the characters and places you chose from the lists. You can provide as much, or as little, detail as you wish.

- When your story is done, reflect on the themes that came up in the story. Think about the characters and settings you chose—did writing your Autobiographical Fairy Tale shed any new light on how you think about your life challenges and/or the people who have played a part in them?

Archetypes and Characters

Queen	Dwarf
King	Troll
Princess	Ogre
Prince	Giant
Servant	Changeling
Baker	Fortune Teller
Blacksmith	Wise Woman
Cobbler	Mermaid
Farmer	Selkie
Hero	Hermit
Villain	Old Crone
Trickster	Superhero
Peasant	Dragon
Suitor	Dragon Slayer
Wizard	Knight
Genie	Soldier
Witch	Warrior
Fairy Godmother	Healer
Father Time	Gypsy
Fairy	Muse
Pixie	Time Traveler
Gnome	Sea Monster
Elf	Minstrel

*

Angel	Bully
Devil	Jester
Cupid	Curmudgeon
Medicine Man or Woman	Wanderer
Shaman	Judge
Dreamer	Monster
Creator	Masquerader
Seer	Tyrant
Gambler	Victim
Alchemist	Martyr
Visionary	Guardian
Inventor	Benefactor
Avenger	Death
Savior	Life
Beggar	Underdog
Hedonist	Damsel in Distress
Messenger	The Grim Reaper
Magician	Ghost
Thief	Spirit
Samaritan	Nymph
Alien	

Fairy Tale Locations

A Castle

An Enchanted Forest

A Haunted Forest

A Crystal Cave

A Village

A Hovel

A Cottage

A Grottel

A Castle Tower

A Dragon's Lair

A Mermaid's Cove

A Royal Ball

A Masquerade Ball

A Field of Flowers

A Giant Beanstalk

The Shadows

Ruins

A Carnival

A Strange Land

A Dungeon

A Labyrinth

A Deserted Island

A Moor

A Bog

An Abbey

A Garden

The End of a Rainbow

A Bridge

A Fairy Land

A Witch's House

A Castle Moat

A Clearing in the Woods

A Marketplace

A Belltower

A Hidden Spring

A Faraway Land

► PAPER HOUSES

Paper Houses is a unique way to document your life story, especially if you've moved more than twice in your life. The goal of the activity is to create "Paper Houses"—individual envelopes labeled with addresses of the places you've lived. Each envelope can be filled with written memories or photos of events that happened at that residence. When you put the houses in sequential order you create a unique timeline of your life.

MATERIALS

Assortment of envelopes—you'll need one envelope for each address where you've lived

Markers and/or ink pens

Paper and pencil

DIRECTIONS

- Make a list of all the places you have lived, whether it was for a few weeks or for years.

- Write one address or location per envelope.

- If you like you can decorate each envelope to resemble what the place looked like. Alternatively, you can draw a map of its location.

- If you have any photos of the place, feel free to put them in the matching envelope.

- Answer any of the following questions and put them in the relevant envelopes as well:

  — What do you remember about how this place looked?

  — How did it smell?

  — What foods did you eat most here?

  — If there were floors, what were the floors like? Were there floorboards? Linoleum? Carpet? Dirt?

  — Did any walls have wallpaper, plaster of Paris, painted walls, or tile? Do you recall specific patterns?

  — Was the place tidy or messy?

  — What was privacy like in this place? How many people shared the space?

— How did sound travel in this place? Where were the best spaces to sing, eavesdrop, or tell secrets?

— Were there any creepy spaces here? What made those spots creepy and unsettling?

— Was the place haunted, or did it carry a certain energy? Were there any stories or legends from this location prior to you living there?

— What age were you while living here? What developmental phases did you reach here? How do you think living here influenced this time of your life?

— Did you "leave your mark" in this house? Were there any places where you caused permanent damage or even created improvements to the place?

— What do you miss, if anything, about this place?

- Describe what your neighbors were like here (if you had any).

- When you've completed this activity put the envelopes in sequential order—the order in which you lived in each place. This creates a visual timeline of your life and where you lived along the way.

▶ METAPHORICAL ME

Metaphors provide a rich landscape of words and images that make describing things, especially yourself, a fun exercise in creative expression. This writing prompt provides an opportunity to describe yourself using metaphors.

MATERIALS

Paper and pencil

DIRECTIONS

- Look at these categories and choose at least three that spark your interest or curiosity:

— animals

— weather phenomena

— types of trees

— elements on the periodic table

— bodies of water

- — shapes
- — vehicles
- — gem stones
- — types of breakfast cereal
- — book titles
- — toys
- — constellations
- — colors
- — cards in a deck
- — famous landmarks
- — types of candy.

- Write your chosen categories on paper.

- Look at the categories you chose. Think about what you would be if you were in each category. For example, if you chose the animal category, what animal would you be?

- Write down your three categories with your corresponding answers. It might look something like this:

  Toy: Yo-Yo

  Animal: Inchworm

  Weather phenomena: Lightning

- Next, expand on your answers by adding one or two details, for example:

  Toy: I am a tangled string on a Yo-Yo.

  Animal: I am an inchworm, slowly but surely reaching my goal.

  Weather phenomena: I'm a bolt of lightning when I get angry. I'm destructive and wild.

- Last, reflect on these metaphors. How did it feel to describe yourself this way?

- If you liked this activity, you can choose additional categories and continue adding to your list.

▶ ARCHETYPAL SELF PORTRAITS

Archetypes are characters that people emulate across the globe. These characters have a significant presence in storytelling, myths, and fairy tales because the personas are familiar to all people regardless of time or culture. If you've ever heard someone say, "He's such an angel," "She's a trickster," "He's a magician," or "She's a witch," then you've already been exposed to the language of archetypes.

For this activity you're invited to create an Archetypal Self Portrait based on one or more archetypes.

MATERIALS

Paper

Pencil

Colored pencils or marker

"Archetypes and Characters" handout

DIRECTIONS

- Refer to the handout titled "Archetypes and Characters" and look over the list of characters.

- Choose one or more archetypes that best describe you.

- Draw a picture of yourself as the archetype/s chosen. If you chose more than one archetype, you can draw them on separate pieces of paper or all together on one page. It's up to you.

- Color them in as desired.

Reflection and/or discussion: Which archetypes did you choose and why? Were there any you wish you could be? Do you think your friends and loved ones would agree with the archetype/s you chose for yourself? Which archetypes do you recognize in your friends and family? Which archetypes would you choose for them?

▶ | AN ANCHOR FOR THE SOUL

"An Anchor for the Soul" is a small, portable box filled with written reminders of who you are. It's a helpful tool to have, especially when you're going through a difficult time or when you're feeling disconnected from yourself. Whenever you need a reminder of who you are—that you are a valued and remarkable human being—you can open your box and view the unique mirror of words and memories that reflect who you are.

MATERIALS

Small, recycled box that has a slide tray inside, e.g. a box for wooden matches or lozenges

Scissors

White or light paper

Sheet of decorative paper

Writing utensils—a pen, thin markers, or colored pencils

Glue

DIRECTIONS

- Remove the tray from the box and set it aside for now.

- Cut a strip of scrapbook paper that can wrap around the outside of the box. You can trace the box onto the paper and then cut a strip of paper the same width.

- Fold the strip of scrapbook paper tightly around the box edges to make sure it will cover the box.

- Apply a thin layer of glue to the underside of the paper strip and then glue it around the outside of the box. Set this part of the box aside to dry.

- Next, work on the sliding tray. Cut one or more long strips of the white or light paper equal to the width of the inside of the tray. The strip of paper will be folded accordion style to fit inside, so do not worry about the length.

- Fold the long strip accordion style so that it fits in the tray. Accordion style means you fold it one direction, then flip it over and fold it in the opposite direction.

- Put the accordion-folded paper strip inside the tray to make sure it fits. If anything needs to be trimmed or fixed, you can do so at this time.

- Look over the categories and questions listed below. Write the categories on the folded strip of paper as well as any answers you want to add. Each category has a list of examples to consider, but you can add whatever is most relevant to your own likes and experiences. If you prefer a more freestyle approach, write or illustrate your answers in random fashion all over the paper.

- Cut and fold additional strips of paper as needed to make room for all you want to include. You can tape the strips together to make one continuous piece if you like.

Scents

List your favorite scents—the ones that fill your heart with positive feelings and fond memories:

Vanilla or cinnamon?

The forest?

The ocean?

Curry?

A certain cologne or perfume?

Coffee?

Your home? Someone else's home?

Rain?

Flowers?

Cut grass?

A new book?

Something cooking on the stove?

Wet mittens in winter?

A new car?

Touch

List your favorite textures and tactile sensations:

Your pet's fur?

A special stuffed animal or blanket?

Someone's hand in yours?

A certain fabric such as corduroy, flannel, silk, or linen?

Rain on your skin?

Getting a massage?

The feel of your toes in warm sand?

Being barefoot?

Clean bed linens?

Soft fluffy slippers?

The rhythm of knitting?

A ripe peach or a slice of watermelon?

Sound

List your favorite sounds:

A loved one's laughter?

A certain song or music?

Rain on the window?

Traffic?

Silence?

A thunderstorm?

Birds singing?

Someone you love singing?

Peeping frogs, cicadas, or crickets on a summer night?

Waves at the beach or other water movement?

An amusement park?

Wind in the trees?

Muses

List your favorite muses, such as:

Artists

Poets

Writers

Performers

Musicians

Philosophers

Pleasure

List your favorite indulgences or "guilty pleasures." Think of the things you would spend your money and time on if there were no barriers to doing so:

Designer clothes or shoes?

Arts and crafts supplies?

Books?

Playing video games for hours?

Watching TV?

Favorite "junk" food?

Favorite "comfort" food?

Spa services, e.g. a massage or facial?

Travel?

Locations and landscapes

Where do you feel most content or happy?

The beach?

At home?

On a mountain?

In the woods?

In bed, snuggling with a pet?

The mall or a store?

At a friend's house?

Someplace you've vacationed or visited that's far away?

A secret hideaway?

On a boat?

An exotic or tropical place?

Unique facts

Name any unique experiences, traits, or talents that you're proud of:

Can you speak other languages?

Can you juggle?

Have you run a marathon?

Can you recite something from memory?

Have you received any awards or special recognition?

Have you published anything?

Have you performed in public?

Have you broken any records?

Do you have any unusual or unique hobbies/pastimes you enjoy?

Have you ever won a contest or lottery?

Have you been skydiving? Scuba diving? Bunging jumping? Rock climbing? Ice climbing?

Quotes

Write down your favorite quotes. Include poems or lyrics that inspire you, make you smile, or remind you of something you need to hear now and then.

Love and kindness

What have been your greatest acts of love or kindness toward others?

Have you ever volunteered?

Have you donated money to a cause?

Have you helped anyone anonymously?

Have you ever sponsored someone for a fundraiser?

Who do you think would thank you for something you have done?

Taste

What are your favorite foods?

Do you have any traditional or family recipes you love to make or eat?

What spices and flavors do you love?

What's your favorite diner meal?

What's your favorite movie food?

What's your favorite candy from childhood or from a candy store?

What are favorite food combinations you love—e.g. apple pie with cheese, ketchup on French fries?

What's your favorite kind of take-out food?

Happy memories

List some of your most treasured, memorable life experiences.

Acts of courage

What are some acts of courage you've experienced?

Have you ever stood up to a bully or abuser?

Sung, performed, or spoken in public?

Listened to your gut feeling rather than follow the crowd?

Ended an unhealthy friendship or relationship?

Gone out to eat or to a movie by yourself?

Travelled alone?

Protested?

Unique experiences

List any odd, miraculous, or magical experiences you've had:

Have you experienced déjà vu?

A near-death experience?

Seen a ghost?

Witnessed a birth?

Been present at a death?

Observed a miracle?

Have you experienced any bizarre coincidences or serendipity?

Listened to your intuition?

Seen astounding beauty in nature?

Visited a healer or shaman?

Had your palms read?

Have you ever saved somebody's life?

Had unbelievable luck?

Survival

Start your sentence with, "I survived…"

Getting struck by lightening?

A form of trauma or violence?

An accident?

A serious injury or illness?

Loss?

Your childhood?

A historical tragedy?

Prejudice or oppression?

Poverty?

Addiction?

- When you've completed your Anchor for the Soul, look it over and make any changes as needed. Reflect on all the amazingly unique details that make you who you are—from the experiences you've had to the personal things you enjoy. Keep your box someplace special where you can access it when it is needed or wanted.

▶ ALCHEMY

Two definitions of alchemy from Merriam-Webster include, "a power or process that changes or transforms something in a mysterious or impressive way" and also "an inexplicable or mysterious transmuting" (Merriam-Webster 2018). Alchemy is usually discussed in terms of medieval science, especially turning common metals into gold. For the purposes of this activity, however, you will be using alchemy as a metaphor for change within yourself that is transformative.

- First, consider a time in your life when something from within you changed as a result of an event or situation. This change could have been in your emotions, beliefs, hopes and dreams, faith, attitude, or worldview.

- Next, reflect on the following:

  - What was the situation or event that happened just prior to this change?

  - What were the very first signs that something within you was changing, or had changed?

  - How and when did others around you start to notice perhaps something about you had changed?

  - What was the final result of the change?

  - What have you lost and what have you gained as a result of the change?

- Draw a "before and after" picture of yourself using the "Alchemy" worksheet.

Alchemy

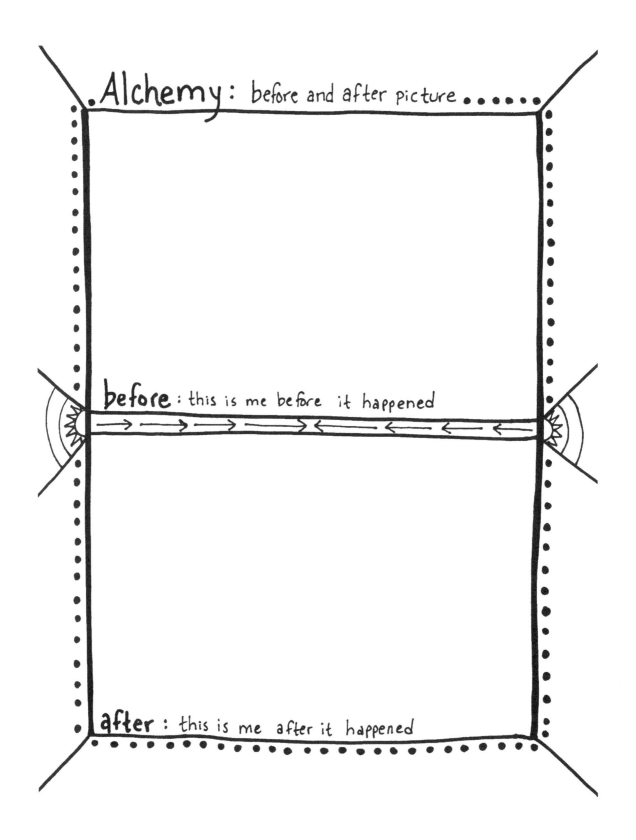

Alchemy: before and after picture

before: this is me before it happened

after: this is me after it happened

▶ FRIENDS AND LOVED ONES IN METAPHOR

This activity provides an opportunity to think about your friends and loved ones using a metaphorical lens—it's a creative and unique way to explore how you view their personalities and their role in your life. For example, if your best friend was a car, what kind of car would they be? How would you answer this?

Use the "Friends and Loved Ones in Metaphor" worksheet to fill out the various metaphors you'd choose for the people on your list.

Friends and Loved Ones in Metaphor

	Person's name:	Person's name:	Person's name:	Person's name:
If this person was a vehicle, what vehicle would they be?				
If this person was an animal, what animal would they be?				
If this person was a plant/tree, what plant/tree would they be?				
If this person was a body of water, which body of water would they be?				
If this person was a color, what color would they be?				
If this person was a movie title, what movie title would they be?				
If this person was a character in a fairy tale, which character would they be?				

5

For Parents

• •

As children reach the tween and teen years they typically seek more independence, which can result in a challenging time to build, or maintain, the connection and relationship you have with them. There are ways to honor their need for independence and still nurture and parent them, however.

The purpose of this chapter is to provide interventions for parents and guardians that encourage such connection. They are interventions I often "prescribe" parents when I'm doing family work involving teens and tweens. This section is brief, but I've chosen the most tried and true activities that get consistent positive feedback.

> First and foremost, however, if you are like many parents who are frequently online or on the phone, shut it off or put it down when your child walks in the room. There is no greater non-verbal message to your child that you're paying attention and you value their presence. This is by far the number one complaint I hear from youth today, that their parents are seemingly more interested in social media/online activity/their phones than their kids.

This chapter starts with an activity called "Letter to Your Younger Self" because it's a means for getting in the mindset of being a tween or teen again. Following this activity are direct interventions for building and maintaining connection with your tweens and teens.

▶ LETTER TO YOUR YOUNGER SELF

I often advise parents to think back to when they were their child's age and to really examine what it was like: what your day-to-day life entailed; who your friends were; what challenges you faced; what you liked about yourself; what you disliked about yourself; what you wished people had known about you then; whether you felt "seen," loved, and heard…or if you felt invisible and neglected; how others perceived you—and if this view was accurate; what your hopes and dreams were at that time; teachers you did and did not connect with, etc.

When you reflect back to this age and consider who you were at the time, what would you tell that younger you now, if you could? What did you need to hear from an adult at that time of your life?

Write a letter from the "adult you" to the "tween/ teen you." Tell your younger self what you needed to hear. Share with yourself whatever information you needed at that time to feel more secure about yourself, your identity, your life, and your worth.

▶ BUILD ON YOUR SHARED INTERESTS

If you and your teen have a shared interest, this can be a wonderful opportunity to explore it together. Most of these ideas require a bit of money or travel, but this is where you have an advantage—teens and tweens typically have limitations on how much money they can spend or how to get from one place to another (as many do), but you may be able to provide an experience they otherwise wouldn't be able to coordinate or afford. Here are some examples:

- If you share a love of sport, see a live game together, watch televised games, watch a documentary about the sport, or celebrate with a favorite meal or dessert when your favorite team wins.

- If you both love a certain food such as Pad Thai, make a point of traveling around your local area (or beyond) to go and sample that food from various establishments. It's a fun opportunity to compare and contrast what you each like about the food from one place to another. If you discover the ultimate Pad Thai, for instance, you now know where to buy it for special occasions, such as when your teen passes their drivers' test.

- If you like the same bands, music, or musicals, attend a concert together, download a newly released album and listen to it (e.g. on a drive or during dinner), go see a musical and/or attend a musical sing-a-long, watch a documentary about the band or musical, or watch a recorded live performance together.

- If you share an interest in cooking or baking, include your child in meal planning and grocery shopping, download new recipes and try them together, take a cooking class together, visit specialty bakeshops to sample new products, or visit food festivals where you can try new and/or local foods.

- If you both enjoy making arts and crafts, get instructions and materials for a craft project you both want to make, shop for art supplies together, go to a paint night event, attend a local art walk, or visit art museums and crafts shows.

▶ COMMIT TO LEARNING ABOUT YOUR CHILD'S UNIQUE INTERESTS

Does your tween/teen have an interest in something that makes no sense to you, or even drives you crazy? If so, you are not alone. Part of a tween/teen's job is to find interests that are unique to them. It's part of the process in separating their identity from their parents/guardians and one that is developmentally appropriate.

So if your tween/teen makes a change in their diet (e.g. "I'm a vegetarian now"), fashion style, music, hobby, religion, etc. it's a wonderful opportunity to learn about these new interests. On the one hand, your teen might want to see you cringe and bristle regarding a new interest of theirs. This, too, is part of the individuation process—it translates to "See? I am different from you."

If they are willing, however, talk to your tween/teen about this interest. What is it they love about it? What does it mean to them? Have they found peers who love the same thing? How do the peers at school or the community respond to them and others who share a passion for this interest?

If your teen is adamant to keep you out of this conversation, you can always explore more about the topic on your own so you have a minimal foundation of knowledge about it. At the very least, being familiar with key terms or expressions about the topic can be helpful.

Sometimes parents ask me what to do when a new interest is possibly concerning. Now and then youth find new interests that raise red flags. The red flags that every parent needs to be aware of are the ones that include (but are not limited to):

- self harm

- extreme changes in personality or behavior

- loss of good friends or peer group

- making impulsive choices that lead to harming self, others, or property

- not showing up for school and/or work

- loss of interest in all—or key—activities

- physical markers of drug and alcohol use/abuse

- withdrawal and isolation from loved ones

- giving prized items away

- acting erratically and out of character.

If you observe any of these red flags, or even if your parental intuition tells you "something feels concerning here," try the following:

- In any situation where you are directly asking your tween or teen a question, be prepared to listen. This is not the time to challenge or argue their feelings and beliefs—it's a time to listen to what they have to say.

- Let your tween/teen know you are concerned.

- Inform them you care very deeply and you're available and willing to help.

- Ask how you can be supportive.

- Ask, "what do you need from me right now?"

- Reach out to the child's guidance counselor or key teachers at school—have they noticed any changes in academic performance or behavior/affect at school?

- If you have a positive relationship with the school, ask for recommendations of community helpers that you can reach out to for added support—this may include support groups, counselors, tutors, alternative education providers, psychiatrists, integrative care providers, etc.

- If your child discloses any safety issues that are of immediate concern (e.g. an active plan for harming self or others), call your local emergency or crisis number.

Overall, however, be prepared for new interests and behaviors to pop up now and then. As long as nothing concerning comes of it, know that your child is exploring their identity and this is a normal developmental process that each of us goes through as we enter young adulthood.

▶ CREATE A WEEKLY RITUAL

If your tween/teen will agree to it, plan a regular weekly time where just the two of you get together for at least 15 minutes to enjoy something lighthearted. For example, it could be having ice cream together on Thursday nights.

If you drive your teen/tween to a weekly appointment, this can also be a good time to add a ritual—e.g. stop at a favorite spot on the way there or back to get a small snack or drink; or prepare drinks to bring with you (e.g. iced herbal teas, smoothies, hot apple cider, hot chocolate).

As a mom of a teen, my weekly ritual has been to get up early Monday mornings to make breakfast for my son before he heads to school. This is an advantageous weekly ritual for a few reasons—it starts his school week on a positive note and with a full stomach. It also gives us a chance to check in about his week ahead.

Keep in mind that weekly rituals do not need to involve a lot of conversation. The most important thing is to be present.

▶ TAKE ADVANTAGE OF DRIVER'S EDUCATION/ LEARNING TO DRIVE TIME

The first several weeks of having a teen in driver's education class can be nerve-wracking, to say the least. At some point your teen will be required to practice driving for a certain number of miles or hours before they can be considered for their actual license. This results in an opportunity to spend time together (if you yourself have a valid driver's license), because you may be one of the few people they can drive with.

Here are some tips for getting through these initial driving hours together:

- If your child is feeling anxious or less confident about driving, plan a route that allows for several places to pull over or park. This will give each of you the opportunity to pause, take a deep breath, shake off the stress, laugh about it, cry about it, and generally just take a break from any tension if needed.

- You can also use these places to take longer breaks, e.g. stop at a local business for refreshments.

- As your teen becomes more confident, this is where you can plan on mini road trips together—your teen is more likely to be motivated about this idea if they have a say in where the road trip destination is. Keep in mind that sometimes you are limited to where your teen can drive, so check online about any laws that may prohibit you from crossing state or country borders. But if you give your teen a budget to plan on, even if it's a few dollars, let them plan a drive where you can have some fun and get a chance to explore together. Some teens appreciate the opportunity to experiment with a budget and an itinerary.

- Finally, if at all possible, make sure to add in extra self care for yourself while your teen is learning to drive. This is a notoriously stressful rite of passage for parents and guardians. Self care and support for yourself is a good investment.

▶ CREATE A JAR OF STARS

I wrote about this activity in my previous book, but it deserves another mention here since it is a project that works beautifully for teens and tweens.

"A Jar of Stars" is a collection of notes written by yourself and others that express words of appreciation, recognition, and encouragement about the recipient. The notes are collected and added to a jar (or even a box) to keep them together. Anytime your child needs a boost of support or needs a reminder that they are loved, seen, and valued, they can look over the notes. It's a project that requires some coordinating and time, but it is well worth it!

DIRECTIONS

- Reach out to people who know and/or appreciate one or more things about your tween/teen. These people might be family, family friends, the teen's friends, relatives, a teacher, a community member, a mentor, etc., and ask them if they are willing to write a "star" for your child. A "star" is a note that includes words of appreciation and admiration for your child's strengths, unique interests, memories shared with the child, etc. Examples include:

"You've taught me so much about football."

"You make me laugh—not many people can do that."

"I admire your ability to remember facts and details."

"Thank you for being your wonderful self."

"I wish I had your determination."

"Your choice in music may drive me crazy, but I do love how passionate you are about the things you love."

"I've always admired the way you include other people."

"Thank you for sticking up for the boy on the bus."

"I heard from your sister that you helped her with her homework—I really appreciate that. Thank you."

"I absolutely love your laugh—it makes me smile every time I hear it."

"I'm so proud of you for studying hard for that test."

"That was so kind of you to open the door for others at the store last Wednesday."

"It took a lot of courage for you to ask your teacher for help—I'm proud of you for that."

- Collect the "stars," including the ones you've written.

- Keep a copy or record of each note in case the jar gets lost or destroyed at some point—you can photograph or photocopy the stars.

- Put the original "stars" in a jar or other container.

- Give the Jar of Stars to the recipient.

- The Jars of Stars can be helpful to the recipients in the following ways:

    — to remind them they are appreciated and loved

    — to remind them they have a community and support system around them

    — to remind them of all the wonderful qualities they have

    — to boost their mood and give them added confidence on days when they need it

    — to remind them they are seen and heard

    — to remind them they have strengths and talents

    — to remind them they are not alone

    — to boost their self esteem.

▶ PRESCRIBE A TRIBE

When children approach adolescence it can be a wonderful opportunity to help them launch toward individuality and independence by "prescribing a tribe." A tribe, in this case, is a small selection of trusted adults that your tween/teen can turn to for various adolescent support. Those adults might include family friends, family, mentors, and trusted adults the child already has a connection with. The idea behind creating a tribe is making sure that your tween/teen has more than you to turn to for support, advice, and encouragement during this key developmental stage.

In general, the stages of creating a tribe look like this:

- First, consider if this is an appropriate support for your child. For example, if your child has experienced a lot of loss in their life, and you don't have any potential tribe members who are consistent and able to commit long term, then Prescribe a Tribe might be more harmful than supportive. You don't want to add more loss to your child's life. Careful consideration needs to be done to make sure this experience is a positive and healthy one.

- Contact safe and trusted adults that you want as part of your child's tribe. Here is an example of what that conversation might look like:

CREATIVE COPING SKILLS FOR TEENS AND TWEENS

"I am reaching out to a number of adults that I respect and admire to see if they are interested in becoming part of _____'s 'tribe.' A tribe in this case is a group of adults who may be of support to _____ in one or more ways, such as troubleshooting adolescent challenges, mentoring, listening, encouragement, etc. Overall, tribe members are people my child could reach out to, other than myself. Some tribe members may want a more active role (e.g. mentoring, going out to coffee now and then to check in) and others will want less of a role. Please be specific about what type of role you'd be interested in providing. The more specific, the better, so we can communicate that to _____. If you are not interested or able to commit to this until _____ turns 18, that is okay. I am really just reaching out to see who is interested in this opportunity at this time. Thank you for your time and please contact me by [insert date] if you would like to discuss this further."

- Wait to see if anyone is interested. If you have no one who is available and able to become part of a tribe, then you stop here, since a tribe is not viable at this time.

- If any or all of the adults have agreed to be part of the tribe, move on to the next phase. Gather formal information such as names and contact information for each tribe member. Also make sure to have specific boundaries defined ahead of time. The list of roles people are willing and able to provide is endless, which is why it's helpful to ask each person specifically what they can and cannot provide:

"Cate is someone you can reach out regarding anything related to art and travel; she would be willing to talk to you about friendships and school, but she has specifically noted she would not feel comfortable discussing alcohol or drug use."

"Jose noted he can help you with applying to colleges, writing resumes, and help with preparing for job interviews."

"Uncle Rick is more than happy to support you with your passion for music—he can bring you to his studio, introduce you to other musicians, or mentor you as you explore opportunities related to your music."

"Our family friend Danielle says you can reach out to her in emergencies of any kind."

- Finalize details about who is committed to the tribe.

- Check in with your tween/teen about the tribe. This may be the first conversation you have with your child about this, and you can describe it much like you did when you reached out to tribe members. If your child is put off about the idea and has no interest in it, follow up with tribe members to let them know your child is unlikely to reach out but they have been given the contact info about the tribe members regardless. Give the list of tribe members and their potential roles to your child so they have it for future reference.

- If your tween/teen is rather intrigued about this tribe, you can follow up in a variety of ways. Have your tween/teen send an introduction and thank you note to each tribe person, just to "open the door." Have a physical gathering or celebration of everyone involved so that everyone can meet each other—this gathering can be as informal or formal as you like (some tweens/teens like the idea of something formal as it feels more like a rite of passage).

- As the tribe coordinator, make sure to have at least annual contact with tribe members to keep the cyclical communication and follow up going.

- Last, step back and let it be. You have provided your child with trusted adults they can turn to for support when needed.

▶ LEARN MORE ABOUT PARENTING INTROVERTS

Introversion, like a lot of traits, can vary. But introverts are people who generally need time alone or in small groups in order to recharge and harness their energy. They can be introspective, observant, and quiet. They tend to have close relationships with a small number of peers.

One challenge for parents who are raising introverts is that our culture doesn't support or nurture their needs. If you've raised an introvert, then you've probably experienced what it's like trying to do all the "normal" activities expected for kids like attending birthday parties, going to public events and gatherings, participating in play groups, attending after-school activities, playing team sports, riding the school bus, etc., whereas many introverted kids prefer time alone, at home, or in small groups.

By now, if you've raised an introvert, you may have connected the dots that your child is an introvert. However, if you're one of the parents still wondering why your tween or teen is less inclined to be active and social "like most kids," then I encourage you to read up on "parenting introverts." Susan Cain has done a beautiful job addressing this topic in two different books titled *Quiet: The Power of Introverts in a World That Cannot Stop Talking* (2013) and *Quiet Power: The Secret Strengths of Introverted Kids* (2017).

When introverted kids hit the tween and teen years, you can support their wellbeing by making sure they have plenty of moments through the week to unwind. Keep a dialogue open about what they personally need in order to manage their own stress levels, and follow through with any support you can provide.

▶ REVERSE LECTURES

A Reverse Lecture is when, instead of reminding your tween/teen of what needs to get done or the rules that need to be followed, etc., you provide an opportunity for them to tell you instead:

"So, you're heading to your friend's house at 5 pm—what needs to get done before you leave?"

"Normally I'd go over all the expectations I have for you tonight—but I'm going to let you tell them to me instead."

"I expect you to be safe and respectful tonight—tell me what that means."

Reverse Lectures might still result in rolled eyes and sighs of frustration from your child, but it gives your child the opportunity to activity engage in the conversation as well as bolster a sense of independence and responsibility. If, or when, your child leaves out a key rule or piece of information, cue them about it.

"What about curfew?"

"And you'll be home when?"

"You'll text me the parent's phone number before you leave, right?"

Reverse Lectures is a strategy to help you and your tween/teen communicate about expectations and responsibilities. If you have the sense of humor and patience, you can also provide your tween/teen the opportunity to Reverse Lecture you as well:

Teen: "You're dropping me off at my friend's house later—what am I going to ask you NOT to do?"

Tween: "My friends said they can come over for pizza tonight. I expect you not to embarrass me—what does that mean?"

▶ PARENT AFFIRMATIONS

Affirmations are messages and reminders we give ourselves to help us through the day. Parenting is a tough job, as you know. There are times when it can feel isolating, overwhelming, and emotionally charged. When you need to calm your mind and spirit, affirmations can provide a calming phrase to focus on. Try practicing any of the following as needed:

I support my child living his/her truth.

I can change when change is needed.

Our home is a place of love.

Our home is a safe place.

Today I will see the very best in my child/children.

Today I will parent from the heart.

I listen to my children.

Today I will talk less and listen more.

Today I will give myself self care and compassion.

I am doing my best.

References

Brody, J.E. (1995) 'Personal health: Beyond ragweed, allergenic combinations.' *The New York Times.* Accessed on 5/13/18 at www.nytimes.com/1995/09/06/us/personal-health-beyond-ragweed-allergenic-combinations.html

Cain, S. (2013) *Quiet: The Power of Introverts in a World That Cannot Stop Talking.* London: Penguin Books.

Cain, S. (2017) *Quiet Power: The Secret Strengths of Introverted Kids.* London: Penguin Life.

Carter, C. (2010) 'What we get when we give.' *Psychology Today.* Accessed on 5/13/18 at www.psychologytoday.com/us/blog/raising-happiness/201002/what-we-get-when-we-give

Carver, L. (no date) '10 powerful mudras and how to use them.' The Chopra Center. Accessed on 5/13/18 at https://chopra.com/articles/10-powerful-mudras-and-how-to-use-them#sm.0000kphdikwhzf4f11in4pqkbfrkl

Chevalier, G., Sinatra, S.T., Oschman, J.L., Sokal, K., and Sokal, P. (2012) 'Earthing: Health implications of reconnecting the human body to the earth's surface electrons.' *Journal of Environmental and Public Health.* Accessed on 5/13/18 at www.hindawi.com/journals/jeph/2012/291541

Chillag, A. (2017) 'Why adults should play, too.' CNN. Accessed on 5/13/18 at www.cnn.com/2017/11/02/health/why-adults-should-play-too/index.html

Clinton, C. (2017) 'MTHFR and children.' Natural Path blog. Available at http://thenatpath.com/experts/mthfr-and-children

Conklin, H.G. (2015) 'Playtime isn't just for preschoolers—Teenagers need it, too.' *Time.* Accessed on 5/13/18 at http://time.com/3726098/learning-through-play-teenagers-education

Department of Environmental Conservation (no date) 'Immerse yourself in a forest for better health.' New York State. Accessed on 5/13/18 at www.dec.ny.gov/lands/90720.html

Frank, P. (2016) 'Study says making art reduces stress, even if you kind of suck at it.' *Huffpost, Culture and Arts.* Accessed on 5/13/18 at www.huffingtonpost.com/entry/study-says-making-art-reduces-stress_us_576183ece4b09c926cfdccac

Grant, B.L. (no date) 'Antidepressant microbes in soil: How dirt makes you happy.' Gardening Know How. Accessed on 5/13/18 at www.gardeningknowhow.com/garden-how-to/soil-fertilizers/antidepressant-microbes-soil.htm

Greenblatt, J.M. (2011) 'Psychological consequences of vitamin D deficiency.' *Psychology Today.* Accessed on 5/13/18 at www.psychologytoday.com/us/blog/the-breakthrough-depression-solution/201111/psychological-consequences-vitamin-d-deficiency

Harvard Health Publishing (2011) *In Praise of Gratitude.* Boston, MA: Harvard Medical School. Accessed on 5/13/18 at www.health.harvard.edu/newsletter_article/in-praise-of-gratitude

Helbert, K. (2016) *Yoga for Grief and Loss: Poses, Meditation, Devotion, Self-Reflection, Selfless Acts, Ritual.* London: Singing Dragon.

Helbert, K. (2013) *Finding Your Own Way to Grieve: A Creative Activity Workbook for Kids and Teens on the Autism Spectrum.* London: Jessica Kingsley Publishers.

Jordan, R. (2015) 'Stanford researchers find mental health prescription: Nature.' Stanford, CA. Accessed on 5/13/18 at https://news.stanford.edu/2015/06/30/hiking-mental-health-063015

Kirkland, C.D. (1992) 'Take an herbal bath: Recommended plants and their properties.' Mother Earth News. Accessed on 5/13/18 at www.motherearthnews.com/natural-health/take-an-herbal-bath-zmaz92amzshe

Koven, S. (2013) 'Busy is the new sick.' boston.com. Accessed on 5/13/18 at http://archive.boston.com/lifestyle/health/blog/inpractice/2013/07/busy_is_the_new_sick.html

Lynch, B. (2018) *Dirty Genes: A Breakthrough Program to Treat the Root Cause of Illness and Optimize Your Health.* New York: HarperCollins. Kindle Edition.

Maurer, R. (2014) 'Don't get rid of your gene for Type II diabetes.' The Blood Code blog. Available at www.thebloodcode.com/dont-get-rid-gene-type-2-diabetes

Mental Health America (no date) 'Dissociation and dissociative disorders.' Alexandria, VA: Mental Health America. Accessed on 5/13/18 at www.mentalhealthamerica.net/conditions/dissociation-and-dissociative-disorders

Merriam-Webster (2018) 'Alchemy.' Accessed on 5/13/18 at www.merriam-webster.com/dictionary/alchemy

Mountain Rose Herbs (2016) 'The healing art of bathing.' Blog. Accessed on 5/13/18 at https://blog.mountainroseherbs.com/herbal-bath-recipes

NHLBI (National Heart, Lung, and Blood Institute) (no date) 'Sleep Deprivation and Deficiency: Healthy Brain Function and Emotional Well-Being.' Bethesda, MD: National Institutes of Health. Accessed on 5/13/18 at www.nhlbi.nih.gov/health-topics/sleep-deprivation-and-deficiency

NIH (National Institutes of Health) Medline Plus (2012) 'Are You Sleep-Deprived? Learn More About Healthy Sleep.' Bethesda, MD: National Institutes of Health. Summer 7(2), 17. Accessed on 5/13/18 at https://medlineplus.gov/magazine/issues/summer12/articles/summer12pg17.html

Niles, F. (2011) 'How to use visualization to achieve your goals.' *Huffpost.* Accessed on 5/13/18 at www.huffingtonpost.com/frank-niles-phd/visualization-goals_b_878424.html

Ober, C., Sinatra, S.T., and Zucker, M. (2010) *Earthing: The Most Important Health Discovery Ever?* Laguna Beach, CA: Basic Health Publications.

Oschman, J.L, Chevalier, G., and Brown, R. (2015) 'The effects of grounding (earthing) on inflammation, the immune response, wound healing, and prevention of chronic inflammatory and autoimmune diseases.' National Center for Biotechnology Information, PMC, *Journal of Inflammation Research.* Accessed on 5/13/18 at www.ncbi.nlm.nih.gov/pmc/articles/PMC4378297

Pedersen, T. (2018a) 'Depersonalization.' Psych Central. Accessed on 5/13/18 at https://psychcentral.com/encyclopedia/depersonalization

Pedersen, T. (2018b) 'Derealization.' Psych Central. Accessed on 5/13/18 at https://psychcentral.com/encyclopedia/derealization

Pillay, S. (2016) *How Simply Moving Benefits Your Mental Health.* Boston, MA: Harvard Medical School. Accessed on 5/13/18 at www.health.harvard.edu/blog/how-simply-moving-benefits-your-mental-health-201603289350

Post Traumatic Growth Research Group (no date) 'What is PTG?' Department of Psychology, University of North Carolina, NC. Accessed on 5/13/18 at https://ptgi.uncc.edu/what-is-ptg

Random Acts of Kindness (no date) 'There are scientifically proven benefits of being kind.' Accessed on 5/13/18 at www.randomactsofkindness.org/the-science-of-kindness

Rankin, L. (2012) 'The healing power of telling your story.' *Psychology Today*. Accessed on 5/13/18 at www.psychologytoday.com/us/blog/owning-pink/201211/the-healing-power-telling-your-story

Seppala, E.M. (2013) '20 scientific reasons to start meditating today.' *Psychology Today*. Accessed on 5/13/18 at www.psychologytoday.com/us/blog/feeling-it/201309/20-scientific-reasons-start-meditating-today

Thomas, B. (2014) *How to Get Kids Offline, Outdoors, and Connecting with Nature: 200+ Creative Activities to Encourage Self-Esteem, Mindfulness, and Wellbeing.* London: Jessica Kingsley Publishers.

Williams, F. (no date) 'This is your brain on nature.' *National Geographic Magazine*. Accessed on 5/13/18 at www.nationalgeographic.com/magazine/2016/01/call-to-wild

Younique Genomics (2015) *Understanding Genomics*. Genomics 101. Toronto, Ontario.